THE

CHRIST

40 OF THE DAYS

THE
CHRIST
OF THE
40 DAYS

A. B. SIMPSON

WHITAKER
HOUSE

Publisher's note: This new edition from Whitaker House has been updated for the modern reader. Some words, expressions, and sentence structure have been revised for clarity and readability. Although the more modern Bible translations quoted in this edition were not available to the author, the Bible versions used were carefully selected in order to make the language of the entire text readily understandable while maintaining the author's original premises and message.

Unless otherwise indicated, all Scripture quotations are taken from the King James Version of the Holy Bible. Scripture quotations marked (NKJV) are taken from the *New King James Version,* © 1979, 1980, 1982, 1984 by Thomas Nelson, Inc. Used by permission. All rights reserved. Scripture quotations marked (AMP) are taken from the *Amplified® Bible,* © 1954, 1958, 1962, 1964, 1965, 1987 by The Lockman Foundation. Used by permission. (www.Lockman.org).

Note: The bold emphasis in the Scripture quotations is the author's.

THE CHRIST OF THE 40 DAYS:
Experiencing the Risen, Triumphant Lord

ISBN: 978-1-62911-018-9
eBook ISBN: 978-1-62911-042-4
Printed in the United States of America
© 2014 by Whitaker House

Whitaker House
1030 Hunt Valley Circle
New Kensington, PA 15068
www.whitakerhouse.com

Library of Congress Cataloging-in-Publication Data (Pending)

1 2 3 4 5 6 7 8 9 10 11 **WH** 21 20 19 18 17 16 15 14

CONTENTS

I

OVERVIEW

"He showed himself alive after his passion by many
infallible proofs, being seen of them forty days, and speaking
of the things pertaining to the kingdom of God."
—Acts 1:3

Easter morning is the beginning of a unique and most tenderly interesting portion of our blessed Savior's life. It is the transition period between His earthly ministry and His heavenly exaltation. Like the Indian summer of the year, there is a tender veil of loveliness and mystery about it that links it with both worlds and makes it an especially appropriate pattern for life *"hid with Christ in God"* (Colossians 3:3), in which we may walk with Him all our days, with our heads in heaven while our feet still tread the earth below. May the Holy Spirit vividly reveal to us such glimpses of this blessed life as will enable us to reproduce it in our own experience and walk with Him with a new sense of His abiding presence and glorious reality!

1. The Christ of the Forty Days Is a Living Christ

This glad resurrection morning dispels from the religion of Jesus all the shadows of the sepulcher and all the morbid atmosphere of sorrow, depression, and death. The Christ of true Christianity is not a bleeding, thorn-crowned *"Ecce Homo"*[1] but a glad and radiant face, bright as the springtide morning and radiant with immortal life. His message is: *"I am he that liveth, and was dead; and, behold, I am alive for evermore"* (Revelation 1:18).

Oh, may this day impress upon our hearts the reality of a risen and living Christ, until He is more actual to us than any other personality, and we know what it means not only to be *"reconciled to God by the death of his Son"* but *"much more [to be] saved by his life"* (Romans 5:10)!

2. The Christ of the Forty Days Is a Victorious Christ

What a picture of easy and uttermost triumph is that resurrection scene! Satan had done his worst, and men had done their best, to hold the Captive in the tomb. But without an effort, the Mighty Sleeper calmly rose before the Easter dawn, deliberately laying off the grave clothes, folding the napkin, and putting all in place as naturally as any of us got dressed this morning. Then, He passed through that colossal stone that closed His tomb without even rolling it aside or breaking the seal. And, before the guards could know that He had risen, He was standing calmly in the garden, talking with Mary as

1. Latin for "Behold the man." (See John 19:5.)

though nothing had happened. Perhaps the most overwhelming impression we have received from all the incidents of His resurrection is the infinite facility with which He put His feet on every foe and rose above every obstacle.

We see the same victorious power expressed in the attitude of the angel who followed Him and who, with a single touch, rolled away the stone from the sepulcher, coolly sat down upon it, and then looked into the faces of the keepers till they grew pale with terror and fled in horror and dismay, without a struggle.

Our risen Christ is still the Mighty Victor over all His foes and ours. If we could see Him now, we would behold Him sitting on His Father's throne, undismayed by all the powers of darkness and *"from henceforth expecting till his enemies be made his footstool"* (Hebrews 10:13). Oh, how it cheers our timid hearts to behold our glorious and victorious Captain and to hear Him say of every adversary and over every difficulty, "I have overcome for you." May God help us to see the Captain as Joshua beheld Him, and before Him the walls of every Jericho will fall and the legions of every opposing force will melt away!

3. The Christ of the Forty Days Is a Simple Christ

How natural, how easy, how simple His manifestations were through those blessed forty days! How quietly He dropped down among the disciples, unheralded, unassuming, unattended by angelic guards, and sometimes undistinguished from them in His simple presence! Look at Him as He meets with Mary in that first morning interview, standing like an ordinary stranger in the garden and speaking to her in easy conversation, *"Woman, why weepest thou? whom seekest thou?"* (John 20:15). And then, when the moment for recognition comes, speaking to her heart in the one simple word of personal and unutterable love that disarmed all her amazement and fear and brought back all the old recollections and affections of her throbbing heart!

See Him again on the way to Emmaus. How naturally He drops in upon the little company as they walk. How unaffectedly He talks with them. How easily He turns the conversation to heavenly themes, and how free from strain His every attitude and word! All they are conscious of is a strange burning in their hearts and a kindling warmth of love. At length they constrain Him, and He allows Himself to be pressed to enter in. He sits down at their table and eats bread as if He had been another disciple like themselves. And only when He vanishes quietly from their sight do they realize, "It is the Lord!"

And yet again on the shores of Tiberias,[2] how exquisite is His approach! How natural His greeting; how easy the mighty miracle of the catch of fish; how calm and unaffected the meeting as they reach the shore; how simple the breakfast in which He Himself takes part. And, how exquisite the interview with Simon Peter, concerning which no words can ever express His delicacy of discrimination and tenderness!

Oh, what a picture of that Blessed One who still lives to be our constant Visitor, our ceaseless Companion and Friend—to meet us like Mary in our hours of sorrow; and to walk with us, as with His disciples, often unrecognized at first; or to greet us in the cold, sad morning, after our long hours of waiting and toil and failure, with His marvelous deliverance and still more gracious words of love and instruction. He is so near that not even our nearest friends can come so close! He is so simple that His messages come as the intuition of our own hearts. And yet He is the Wonderful Counselor and the Mighty God for all our perplexities and all our hard places. Oh, blessed Christ of the Forty

---

2. The Sea of Galilee.

Days, help us to walk with You with a faith more simple and a love more childlike!

4. The Christ of the Forty Days Is a Mighty Christ

It is hard for us to realize the Presence that comes with such gentle footsteps and undemonstrative simplicity. Yet behind that gentle form and those noiseless steps is the Omnipotence who could say, *"All power is given unto me in heaven and in earth"* (Matthew 28:18).

All power is His in heaven. He is the Lamb in the midst of the throne who holds in His hand the seven seals and unrolls the scroll of destiny and providence for all worlds, beings, and events. All the mighty acts of God recorded in the Old Testament were but manifestations of His power. All the mighty movements that began with His ascension are the workings of His hands. All the movements of divine providence are subject to His command. All the mighty angels of heaven's myriad hosts are subject to His bidding. All the powers of hell tremble at His name! All the promises of God are fulfilled with His endorsement. All the laws of nature are subject to His mandates.

And all power on earth is subordinate to His power. No wind can blow without His permission, no disease can strike except as He allows. No human hand can hurt us while He shields us with His presence. The circumstances of our lives, the enemies of our souls, and the infirmities of our bodies are subject to His word. Moreover, the very thrones of earth are subordinate to His authority. He can make a Cyrus send back the tribes of Israel by a national decree. He can make a Constantine behold the flaming cross upon the sky and become a follower of the heavenly standard. He can open nations and kingdoms to the gospel, and so He bids us to go forth and disciple all the nations because of His almighty power on our behalf!

All power on earth is subordinate to Jesus' power.

How mighty the power of the resurrection! It surmounted the power of death and the grave; it passed through the solid stone; it defied the stamp of the Roman government and the sentinels of the Roman army. It could pass through the closed doors without rending them asunder. It could bring the miraculous catch of fish to the apostle's net with a single word of command. It could rise without an effort in the chariot of His ascension. It could anoint those weak and timid men with the power that shook the world and laid the foundations of the church.

Oh, that our eyes were but opened so that we might behold the riches of the glory of our inheritance and the exceeding greatness of His power that was worked in Christ when God raised Him from the dead and set Him at His own right hand in heavenly places, far above all principality and power and might and dominion, and every name that is named, and gave Him to be Head over all things to the church, which is His body. (See Ephesians 1:18–23.) Why is it that we do not receive and realize more of this almighty Christ? Alas, it is because we cannot understand or stand the fullness of His power! God is ready to work through us the triumphs of His omnipotence, but we must be fit vessels, open to His touch and able to stand His power. The ordinance that has to bear a mighty charge of powder must be heavy enough to stand the charge without explosion. And so, the heart that is to know the power of Him who *"is able to do exceeding abundantly above all that we ask or think"* (Ephesians 3:20), must be *"strengthened with might by his Spirit in the inner man*" (Ephesians 3:16), so that Christ may dwell in that heart by faith. (See Ephesians 3:17.) To think of what Christ is ready and willing to do in us and for us would frighten some of us into apoplexy, and actually to realize it would snap the frail thread of life itself. Christ's heart is bursting with resources that the world needs, and that He is ready to use, if only He could find vessels ready and willing to use them.

Oh, for the courage to see the power that He is waiting to place at the service of all who are consecrated enough to use it for His glory and close enough to receive the heavenly baptism! He has for us the power of the Holy Spirit, the power of prayer, the power that will conquer circumstances and control all events for His will, and the power that will make us the trophies of His grace and the monuments of His indwelling presence and victory.

We will find this power as we go forth to use it according to His own commission, "*Go ye therefore, and teach* [disciple] *all nations*" (Matthew 28:19). Nothing but a work as wide as the world can ever make room for the power that Christ is waiting to bestow.

5. The Christ of the Forty Days Is a Loving Christ

How unavailing all His power would be if we were not sure that it is available for us, and that His heart loves us as tenderly as His mighty hand can help us. How tender and loving is the Christ of the Forty Days! See Him in the garden as He speaks to Mary with tender sympathy, "*Woman, why weepest thou? whom seekest thou?*" (John 20:15), and then calls her by her name in tones that must have expressed more than words can tell. What mourner can doubt henceforth His sympathy and love? What heart can hesitate to accept His friendship, which still speaks to each of us with as direct and personal a call, and gives to each a name of special and affectionate regard?

Or look at him again as He meets with Thomas, the doubting one, the willful disciple who petulantly demanded that the Lord should give him evidence that He had given to none other, and that no human heart had a right imperiously to claim. But how tenderly the Lord concedes even his demand, until Thomas is ashamed to accept it. More amazed at his Lord's magnanimity and omniscience than at the evidence of His wounds, he cries, *"My Lord and my God"* (John 20:28). One who is harassed by doubts and difficulties does not need to fear again to bring them to the presence of Him who, with such condescending love, is ready to meet them all and to make our hearts know, by the deeper evidence of His own great love and the revealing of Himself, that He is indeed the Son of God.

And look at His conversation with Simon Peter! No backslider ever needs to doubt again the Savior's forgiving love, or fear to come and know that he will be welcomed to a nearer place in His heart and a higher service in His kingdom if only he can say, as Simon said, *"Lord, thou knowest all things; thou knowest that I love thee"* (John 21:17).

So tender, so forgiving, so full of love He comes to us to dry our tears, to satisfy our doubts, to forgive our failures, to restore our souls, and then to use us for a higher service, because we have learned through our own infirmities the depths of His great love. The secret to walking closely with Christ and working successfully for Him is to fully realize that we are His beloved.

Let us but feel that He has set His heart upon us; that He is watching us from those heavens with the same tender interest that He felt for Simon and Mary; that He is working out the mystery of our lives with the same solicitude and fondness; that He is following us day by day like a mother follows her baby in his first attempt to walk alone; that He has set His love upon us; and, in spite of ourselves, is working out for us His highest will and blessing, as far as we will let Him. Then, nothing can discourage us. Our hearts will glow with responsive love. Our faith will spring to meet His mighty promises. And our sacrifices will become the very luxuries of love for One so dear. This was the secret of John's spirit. *"We have known and believed the love that God hath to us"* (1 John 4:16). And the heart that has fully learned this has found the secret of unbounded faith and enthusiastic service.

6. The Christ of the Forty Days Is a Physical Christ

He who came forth alive from Joseph of Arimethea's tomb came forth in the flesh, with a material body and the same form that He had laid down in death and the grave. Jesus made this point most emphatic in His meeting with His disciples after His resurrection. He wanted them to be thoroughly assured that there was no illusion about His body. *"Handle me, and see"* were His emphatic words, *"for a spirit hath not flesh and bones, as ye see me have"* (Luke 24:39).

Indeed, His spiritual consciousness had not died; it was His body alone that tasted death, and it was His body therefore that was raised from death. The resurrection of Christ, then, is a physical fact, and the physical meaning of the resurrection must be of surpassing importance. It means no less than this: that He has come forth to be the physical life of His people now, and, in a little while, the Fountain of their immortality and the Head of their resurrection bodies.

What a source of strength and inspiration it is for us to know that our blessed Lord still has the same physical organization that we possess and is willing and able to share with these mortal frames His infinite and quickening life! He is our living Bread, and, as He lived by the Father, so we may live by Him. Not only is He the source of health and strength to our material life, but He cares for the needs of the body.

His disciples were hungry and cold with their fruitless fishing that Galilean morning, and He saw their need and tenderly asked them, *"Children, have ye any meat?"* (John 21:5). And then, filling their empty nets and spreading the table on the shore, He said, *"Come and dine"* (John 21:12). Thus, He still thinks of the poor and the struggling, the hungry and the helpless. He stands beside us in our need, ready and able by a word to provide immediate and abundant supply.

Jesus is our living Bread. As He lived by the Father, so we may live by Him.

Are we today in any place of need? The Christ of the Forty Days is nearer than we think, able to be *"touched with the feeling of our infirmities"* (Hebrews 4:15) and ready to give us the greatest help in time of need. Like the fishers of yonder sea, our empty nets can be filled at His bidding. The perplexed workman can be directed to the very thing to do; the wretched failure can be altogether corrected.

There is no need that He cannot supply, no counsel that He is not able to give, no regions where His power does not penetrate, no disciple that He does not love to help in every time of need. Oh, let us trust Him more with all our circumstances and sorrows, and our utmost need will only prove even more the infinite resources of His love and grace.

7. The Christ of the Forty Days Is Ever Present

The Christ of the Forty Days is not a transient vision that has passed away forever but rather the Christ of all the ages. Standing at the close of those blessed days midway between earth and heaven, we hear Him say, *"Lo, I am with you always, even to the end of the age"* (Matthew 28:20 NKJV). That blessed present tense has bridged the past and the present and has prolonged those heavenly days after the resurrection through all the days since then. It is not "I will be," as one who has to go away and come back again but *"I am,"* as a presence that is never to be withdrawn.

Jesus says, in effect, "It is true that I am unseen, but I am to remain among you as real in My absence as I am now in My presence." For, in the spiritual world, distance and time are eliminated. And, just as the telescope can bring the distant object near to the eye, and the telephone can present the voice hundreds of miles away to the listening and attentive ear, so there is a spiritual mechanism that can make Christ as immediate to our hearts as if He were visibly by our side. If we had but another sense, all heavenly beings and realities would be directly present to our perception.

The promise of this beautiful passage is not fulfilled only in the presence of Christ in the heart of the believer, which is a literal and glorious truth, but it is a presence *with us*. It is more than the spiritual consciousness of the Lord's indwelling. It is His direct personality and constant companionship with our entire life, and His omnipotent cooperation in all our needs. It is the presence of One who has all power in heaven and in earth and whose presence means the defeat of every adversary, the solution of every difficulty, the supply of every need.

In these days, it does seem as though we could almost see Him moving in the midst of His people, here and there, in His mighty working—on the mission field with the lone worker; in the midst of dangers and foes; in the busy streets of the crowded city; in the mingled incidents of business life; in the whirl and confusion of our intense life today; in every department of human society—touching with His hands all the chords of influence and power, moving the wheels of providence, and working out His purpose for His people and the redemption of the world.

Oh, once more, that we might see Him as Joshua saw the Captain when he entered Canaan and camped around Jericho; as Stephen saw Him when he faced the crowd of wolfish foes that thirsted for His blood; as Paul saw Him amid the tempests of the Adriatic and the lions of the Colosseum; as John saw Him walking in the midst of the seven golden candlesticks, holding in His hand the seven stars, standing in the midst of God's throne, and then standing before the throne with all the seals of human destiny in His own right hand! Then, indeed, no trial could discourage us, no foe intimidate us, no fear dismay us, no work overwhelm us; for above every voice of peril or of hostile power, we would hear His gentle whisper, *"Lo, I am with you always* [*"all the days"* AMP], *even to the end of the age"* (Matthew 28:20 NKJV).

It is correctly translated *"all the days,"* not *"always."* He comes to us each day with a new blessing. Every morning, day by day, He walks with us, with a love that never tires and a blessing that never grows old. He is with us *"all the days"*; it is a ceaseless abiding. There is no day so dark, so commonplace, so uninteresting, that you will not find Him there. Often, no doubt, He is unrecognized, as He was on the way to Emmaus, until you realize how your heart has been warmed, your love stirred, and your Bible so strangely vivified that every promise seems to speak to you with heavenly reality and power. It was the Lord!

May God grant that His living presence may henceforth be made more real to us all. And whether we have the consciousness and evidence, as Jesus' disciples had a few glorious times in those forty days, or whether we go forth into the coming days as they did most of the time, to walk by simple faith and in simple duty, let us know, at least, that the fact is true forevermore that *He is with us*, a Presence unseen but real, and ready at any moment if we should need Him to manifest Himself for our relief.

There is a beautiful story about the mother of an English schoolboy. When he was a lad, she sent him to a boarding school some distance from her home, where the rules of the school permitted her to visit him only once a fortnight. But it was more than this mother's heart could stand, and so, completely unknown to her boy or his teachers, she rented a little attic overlooking the school. She would often sit in that upper room with her eyes on her darling boy as he played in the yard below or studied in the schoolroom. He could not see her, nor did he dream that she was there, but if he had cried or called her name, or needed her for a moment, he was within her reach.

This is a little parable of the sleepless love and ceaseless oversight that our Savior exercises toward His beloved ones. For He has His eye upon us by day and by night; and, although we do not see His face and hands and form as He moves through our pathway, dissipating our foes and clearing our way, yet He is there, always there "[*"all the days"* AMP], *even unto the end*" (Matthew 28:20). Let us believe His promise, let us assume the reality of His presence, let us recognize Him as always near, let us speak to Him as One always by our side, and He will always answer us, either by the whispers of His love or by the workings of His hand.

Thus we will never be alone; thus we will never be defenseless; thus we will never be defeated; thus we never need to fear. And even if the lonely vale itself opens to us, it will be but the opening vista of a larger vision and a closer and nearer Presence, as we find that *"neither death, nor life, nor angels, nor principalities, nor powers, nor things present, nor things to come, nor height, nor depth, nor any other creature, shall be able to separate us from the love of God, which is in Christ Jesus our Lord"* (Romans 8:38–39).

2

THE FIRST WEEK: THREE MEETINGS

Let us linger, in simple meditation and daily fellowship with Jesus, upon the scenes and incidents of the forty days. We will look at the three most prominent incidents of the first week after the resurrection. They all occurred on the first day of the week, the resurrection Sabbath. The first was the conversation with Mary Magdalene in the garden in the early morning; the second, the walk with the two disciples in the afternoon; and the third, the appearing to the eleven disciples as they waited in the upper room in the evening. Each has its own special lessons—lessons that will help us to realize more vividly the presence of Him who is still with us "[*all the days*" AMP], *even to the end of the age*" (Matthew 28:20 NKJV).

The Morning Meeting with Mary Magdalene

1. Christ Knows Each of Us by Name

This meeting reveals to us a Christ who knows each one of us by name. The most marked feature of this entire conversation is the individuality of Jesus' recognition. Two persons are very distinctly present. There is no doubt about the personality of Christ, and there is no doubt about His personal love for Mary Magdalene. It is true that she was not immediately prepared to recognize Him and receive His greeting. But the moment she was ready, His heart was overflowing with one, all-comprehending word, *"Mary"* (John 20:16)! (See John 20:11–18.)

Such a Christ we still have. He calls each of us by name, and amid the myriads of the universe and of His own, He knows us apart and loves us for ourselves. May the Lord help us to fully realize this soul-inspiring consciousness, that each one of us is something to Jesus, everything that we will let Him make us! His heart to us today is waiting only for the "Amen" of responsive trust. He says, *"Yea, I have loved thee with an everlasting love: therefore with lovingkindness have I drawn thee"* (Jeremiah 31:3). Let us go forth to write our name, "The Disciple Whom Jesus Loved."

2. Christ Is Revealed to Us as a Spiritual Presence

The meeting with Mary also makes known the Christ who is henceforth to be revealed as a spiritual presence rather than a bodily presence. This is the meaning of the caution, *"Touch me not; for I am not yet ascended to my Father: but go to my brethren, and say unto them, I ascend unto my Father, and your Father; and to my God, and your God"* (John 20:17). This seems to be intended as a gentle hint to her that she is not to recognize Him and embrace Him too eagerly in the earthly way but to learn to know Him as a spiritual presence and as the Ascended One by a touch that can reach Him through all the intervening spaces and in the absence of His visible form.

Even when Jesus walked the earth, there were two touches by which men came in contact with Him. There was the touch of mere physical approach. Peter referred to this when the multitude thronged Christ, and He asked, "*Who touched me?*" (Luke 8:45). Peter answered, in effect, "Why, the multitude all touch You and throng You." "But," said Christ, "*somebody hath* **touched** *me*" (Luke 8:45–46). Christ meant another sort of touch, the touch of faith and spiritual recognition. And this was the touch to which He was educating Mary now, because it was to be the way of contact in the coming ages between Him and His people, the contact that we all may have with Him now.

It is very doubtful that Jesus Christ appeared after His resurrection to anyone who did not know Him spiritually. And, if He were to come to us today in His mere natural, physical presence, it is doubtful if it would be a real help to our spiritual communion. It would rather distract us from that deeper inner union and fellowship that we have with Him in spirit, and awaken merely our outward senses to recognize Him. If He were to be perpetually with us in this external aspect, the inner senses that recognize Him would become enervated and paralyzed for lack of exercise, and we would, in our present state, really be separated from the Lord in His highest character and attributes. Therefore, it was expedient for the disciples that He should go away, in order that the Comforter might come and lead them into the higher spiritual capacity and communion. (See John 16:7.)

This was what Christ was unfolding to Mary, and this is what we need to understand if we want to have deep and ceaseless communion with our Lord. When we have been made perfect in this spiritual relationship, then we will pass into a higher physical communion, corresponding to His own resurrection body, and, with all the senses of our inner and outer being, we will apprehend and enjoy Him forever. It is the lack of this higher touch that makes it so difficult for many to receive the healing of the Lord, but it is as true as ever that as many as touch Him are made perfectly whole. (See, for example, Matthew 14:35–36.)

3. Christ Is Identified with Us in Unity, Brotherhood, and Partnership

Additionally, this incident reveals a Christ who is identified with us in the most perfect unity and brotherhood and who receives us into partnership with all His rights and relationships to the Father. He said, "*Go to my brethren, and say unto them, I ascend unto my Father, and your Father; and to my God, and your God*" (John 20:17). These are wonderful words; higher, perhaps, than we have dreamed. It is a great thing to know that we are the sons of God, but it is a greater thing to know that we are the sons of God even as Jesus is. It is not simply that we are created and born into a sonship in the Father's house, but, by union with Him, we are received into *His sonship* with the Father, and, looking in the face of God, can say, "His Father and my Father, His God and my God."

Let us fully realize and not shrink from the stupendous meaning of these words. The very relationship that Jesus sustains with His Father, He has given to us along with Himself. And, to make it good, He has given to us His own nature, His divine nature, in the measure in which we can receive it. Therefore, with the very nature and love of God Himself within us, it is true of us that "*both he that sanctifieth and they who are sanctified are all of one: for which cause he is not ashamed to call them brethren*" (Hebrews 2:11).

He is the Son of God as no angel or other created being can ever be, the only begotten Son of God, but it is this sonship that He shares with us. And so we are called, in that wonderful passage in Hebrews, the "firstborn ones." (See Hebrews 12:23.) We are all recognized, not as younger sons, sustaining a lower relationship with the Father, but as firstborn ones, because our sonship is inherited from the Firstborn and Only Begotten.

Let no one be startled, as though this was claiming equality with God. No single believer is equal with Christ, but every true disciple is part of the whole body of Christ, and the whole body is one with the Head and filled with all His fullness. No single one of us can hold all the fullness of Christ, but the whole body of the redeemed will hold it all; and Christ will appear throughout eternity, not apart from us but as a part of us and we of Him. We do not have mere resemblance to Christ but identity with Christ, and joint heirship with Him of God and of all His fullness. Therefore, Jesus says, even of His Father's love, *"The love wherewith thou hast loved me may be in them, and I in them"* (John 17:26).

What is the practical meaning of all this? It is manifold and marvelous. It means that our standing and acceptance are as complete as His own. It means that we may pray in His name so that it will be even as if He were praying—not we. It means that all His righteousness, nature, and personal attributes may be imparted to us and appropriated by us, so that He Himself will literally live in us. It means that we are entitled to all His strength and life. It means that we inherit all His glory and will sit with Him on His throne as He sat down on His Father's throne. Oh, it is this that makes our love perfect, even in the day of judgment, *"because as he is, so are we in this world"* (1 John 4:17)!

*We do not have mere resemblance to Christ
but identity with Christ, and joint heirship with Him
of God and of all His fullness.*

Beloved, let us listen to the echoes of that message from the resurrection morning that Jesus bade Mary tell us all, *"My Father, and your Father;...my God, and your God"* (John 20:17), until from the Father's lips it whispers back to the rejoicing heart, *"Son, thou art ever with me, and all that I have is thine"* (Luke 15:31).

The Walk to Emmaus

It is the afternoon of the same bright Sabbath. Two simple-hearted men, who had been the friends of Jesus, are walking from Jerusalem to a little village in the country and talking of the things that have recently come to pass in connection with Him. Soon they are conscious of a third Person who has incidentally joined them. There is nothing in His manner to awaken special interest until He begins to talk with them about the theme of their conversation, and He gradually leads the discussion awhile as He opens up to them, as an intelligent rabbi might be expected to do, the Old Testament Scriptures concerning the Messiah.

Still, all they are conscious of is a warmth in their hearts as the light begins to break on their spiritual understanding. They are strongly drawn to their new Companion, and as they reach the gate of their little home, they earnestly press Him to tarry with them under their humble roof. He consents, and, going in, sits down with them to their evening meal. The risen Christ still acts as the stronger spirit, and they allow Him to preside and bless the bread before they eat. But lo! as He breaks the bread before them, the spell that had bound their vision from recognizing Him is broken, and suddenly they behold in His face the old light and expression of Jesus of Nazareth. It grows bright with the halo of His heavenly glory for a moment, and then He vanishes out of their sight, and they look at one another with amazement and joy, knowing that it was the Lord. (See Luke 24:13–32.)

How we thank the dear Master for that scene! How near it has brought Him to our lives. How simple it has made His coming and communion. How glorious to know that He *"is the same yesterday, today, and forever"* (Hebrews 13:8 nkjv)!

1. Jesus Comes to Us Incidentally and Casually in All Walks of Life

This meeting teaches us of the incidental and casual coming of our Lord to us in all walks of life. It was no set appointment. Jesus just dropped down beside them and entered, without introduction, into their simple conversation. And He is still willing to come into the ordinary interactions of our life. He is really with us in the workshop, in the kitchen, and along the busy street. It is not necessary that we should be illustrious and especially important, for those two disciples whom He thus honored are little known. The name of only one of them is given us (see Luke 24:18), and this one cannot be certainly identified; the other we do not even possess sufficient light to speculate about. Thank God that we do not know them, for it hints to us that the most obscure and commonplace of God's children may count upon the recognition and companionship of Jesus in the most commonplace circumstances of their life.

> The busy mart, the communion task,
> May furnish all we ought to ask;
> Room to deny ourselves—a road
> To lead us daily nearer God.

2. Jesus May Often Be with Us Unrecognized

Jesus was with these disciples but went unrecognized by them. This is not spoken of as their fault. We are told that *"their eyes were holden"* (Luke 24:16) so that they could not know Him, and, later, that *"their eyes were opened, and they knew him"* (Luke 24:31). There is much precious significance in this. The Lord is often present in our lives in things that we do not dream possess any significance. We are asking God about something that needs His mighty working, and the very instrument by which He is to work is by our side, perhaps, unrecognized for weeks and months and years until, suddenly, one day it grows luminous and glorious with the very presence of the Lord and becomes the mighty instrument of His victorious working. He loves to show His hand through the unexpected. Often, He keeps us from seeing His way until just before He opens it, and then immediately it is all unfolded, and we find that He was walking by our side in this very thing long before we even suspected its meaning.

Jesus wants us to recognize His presence where we cannot see it and where nothing seems to speak of it, but everything around us is ordinary and human. Oh, it is in the faces and forms that seem just as ordinary to us as His did to them that the Lord is often nearest to us. Let us therefore walk henceforth as though every sound was the footfall of His steps and every person the embodiment of Himself!

3. Christ May Always Be Recognized by His Word

This meeting also teaches us of a Christ who may always be recognized by His Word. For it was thus that He spoke to them. He might have told them of much besides that. For example, He might have brought back with Him the secrets of the under-world, from which He had just come, but He gave no hint of its awful mysteries. He might have amazed them by some picture of the celestial country to which He was going so soon, but He did not attempt to dazzle them with such visions. He might have poured out some marvelous teachings like His own incomparable parables. But no! He simply takes the old Bible and interprets it in the light of the very things of which they had been speaking—His own death and resurrection. *"And beginning at Moses and all the prophets, he expounded unto them in all the scriptures the things concerning himself"* (Luke 24:27).

Thus, beloved, we can all have His fellowship still, and thus we can always test every revelation and every mystery. Does it correspond with the Scriptures, and does it speak of the things concerning Himself? How wonderful it must have been to hear Him expound on the sacrifice of Abel, the offering up of Isaac, the brazen serpent, the Paschal Lamb, and all the wondrous types that speak so eloquently of Him! So, still, He is willing to talk with us and make the Bible live and shine with heavenly illumination and vividness, until our hearts burn within us.

It is thus that the presence of Jesus is revealed. The Bible becomes a new book, a book for our hearts, and a book full of our living Savior. Oh, that He may come to us and thus open to us its deeper mysteries of life and truth and its meaning for our generation and our own life and work. For this book is something to you that it is not to another, and something for our day that it never was to the world before; and, in order to make it so, we must have the living Christ Himself open it to us and open our understanding to receive its light.

4. Christ Manifests Himself to Us

This incident teaches something more than even the precious word of Christ, for it tells us of His actual manifestation to the disciples. As He blessed and broke the bread, *"they knew him"* (Luke 24:31). Oh, there is such a thing as this—the actual revealing of Christ in His personality to the soul until it knows for itself, with a consciousness that none can deny, that He has been there. It is not simply the consciousness of His presence in the heart by the Holy Spirit, for this we may always have. But there is a direct revealing of Christ as a Presence greater than our hearts, or all hearts—a Presence that sometimes is especially made manifest for His own wise purpose to the tried or waiting heart. Sometimes, He comes a little nearer in His own glorious majesty and makes the spirit feel that He has passed by in all His ascended glory and laid His hand upon us and done something for us as mighty as His own omnipotence.

He sometimes came to the apostles in this way. Such was that day when He visited Paul, who was on the way to Damascus, and conquered him by a look and a word of love, and then sent him forevermore on his new and heavenly way, a flaming torch of light and love. (See Acts 9:1–31.) So, too, He came in His great life work, occasionally, in hours of crisis, to the apostle and made him understand that the Master had been there for a brief moment and had spoken the decisive word that turned the course of all the coming years.

He came to Paul in this way at Corinth in the moment of his depression and said, *"Be not afraid,…for I am with thee, and no man shall set on thee to hurt thee: for I have much people in this city"* (Acts 18:9–10). So, again, He came to him in that dark hour when he had just passed through the awful scenes of his arrest in Jerusalem and his trial before the Sanhedrin, and said, *"Be of good cheer, Paul: for as thou hast testified of me in Jerusalem, so must thou bear witness also at Rome"* (Acts 23:11). So, again, on the Adriatic sea, in that wild hurricane, He stood for a moment on the midnight deck and gave the word that brought all that crew safely to land. (See Acts 27.) When Paul was in the court of Nero, all the believers forsook him (see 2 Timothy 4:16), but, he later reported, *"The Lord stood with me, and strengthened me"* (2 Timothy 4:17). Paul was also put in the Colosseum, but he could testify, as well, *"I was delivered out of the mouth of the lion"* (2 Timothy 4:17).

So, still, Jesus comes to us at times, just for a moment, perhaps, but that moment is enough to heal our bodies from the wreck of disease, to rescue us from some hour of extremity or peril, or to cover all the future with blessing and power. He knows when we need the mighty visitation. We may not see it with our physical eyes, but our soul will be conscious that He has passed by, that things can never again be as they were before, and that over all our life is written *Jehovah Shammah*.[3] This is a blessed promise for every loving disciple. Lord, help us to claim it for ourselves; and make it real to every one of us. *"He that hath my commandments, and keepeth them, he it is that loveth me:…and I will love him, and will manifest myself to him"* (John 14:21).

5. The Manifestation of Christ's Special Presence Is Transient

This incident also teaches us that the manifestation of Christ's special presence is transient and is speedily withdrawn. The moment the disciples recognize Him, He vanishes out of their sight. Had He lingered, they would have been thrown off the former plane of faith and disarmed for the simpler walk to which He called them. One glimpse was enough for the present, and in the memory of that look they must walk in simple trust, even as the mariner on the voyage catches one glimpse of the star and sails by that one glimpse for days on the pathless sea. *"For we walk by faith, not by sight"* (2 Corinthians 5:7), and *"though now [we] see him not, yet believing, [we] rejoice with joy unspeakable and full of glory"* (1 Peter 1:8).

---

3. "The Lord is there."

The Meeting in the Upper Room

The meeting in the upper room is the sequel to the afternoon meeting and follows close upon it. It is intended, therefore, to teach still further lessons about the risen Lord. Both Luke and John record this incident of the evening of the first day of Jesus' resurrection. Through the closed doors of the upper room, Jesus quietly entered. Spreading out His hands in benediction, He twice repeated the gracious word, *"Peace be unto you"* (John 20:19, 21). He added, *"As my Father hath sent me, even so send I you"* (John 20:21), and, breathing upon them said, *"Receive ye the Holy Ghost"* (John 20:22). In this meeting, also, He made His physical identity very real and certain to their doubting hearts. *"He showed unto them his hands and his side"* (John 20:20) and ate among them as formerly. (See Luke 24:41–43.) From this delightful incident, we learn the following truths, for our comfort.

1. The Risen Christ Has Physical Life and a Body

Jesus Christ has physical life and a real body just like our own, with every member and organ complete, even in His glorified humanity. This fact gives intense reality to the conception of our Lord. He is no shadowy apparition but actual flesh and even bones that could partake of food and that the disciples could handle and see. This body was the real subject of the resurrection, for Jesus' spirit had never died; and this body is the type and pledge of our resurrection in the body, and the source of that physical healing that we now may draw from Him as the foretaste and earnest of our own future resurrection.

2. The Risen Christ's Body Is Infinitely Spiritualized and Exalted

We learn, also, that Jesus' body is infinitely spiritualized and exalted above even its former state. It is the same body, but it is unspeakably finer, mightier, and more glorious. Similarly, the same piece of steel may be refined from an ordinary nail into an exquisite hairspring, but it is still the same metal. Not only this, but it could even be converted into vapor by a chemical process; however, it would still have the property of matter. It could become intangible to the touch and invisible to the eye, and be simply an ethereal fluid, and then it could be transformed again into a solid state. We know yet but little about the convertibility of matter, and what we do know is a coarse illustration—almost unworthy of the subject before us—of Christ's body. We may not understand all the properties of the resurrection, but let us reverently believe the simple facts and believingly receive the life of our glorious Head, who has made us *"members of his body, of his flesh, and of his bones"* (Ephesians 5:30).

3. The Risen Christ Gives Peace

The Christ of this beautiful picture is the Messenger of Peace to our troubled hearts. The secret of rest is to receive the risen Christ and accept His twofold peace. First, peace with God on the grounds of His complete atonement. Second, *"the peace of God, which passeth all understanding"* (Philippians 4:7), through His indwelling presence as the rest for our troubled hearts.

4. The Risen Christ Gives Power

The gift of the Living One is not only peace but power. *"He breathed on them, and saith unto them, Receive ye the Holy Ghost"* (John 20:22). This was the beginning of Pentecost but not its fullness. We must always receive the fullness of the Comforter from the lips of Jesus, even as His very breath. And so He waits to breathe on each of us, as often as He touches us, the fresh anointing of the very same Spirit who dwelt in Him and who comes to us colored, softened, and sweetened by His indwelling in the blessed Jesus and as the very Spirit of Jesus. This is our power; and this power may be received only by appropriating faith, as well as by the faithful appropriation of the power to His service and glory.

Jesus waits to breathe on each of us the fresh anointing of the very same Spirit who dwelt in Him.

---

5. The Risen Christ Gives His Great Commission

Of course, the great commission for service accompanies the promise and touch of power. *"As my Father hath sent me, even so send I you"* (John 20:21). Indeed, this is the great object of all the manifestations of the risen Christ. To each of the disciples, He either directly gives, or at least intimates, the same great obligation to bear to others the blessing that they cannot keep for themselves without losing it. Oh, let us realize that this Christ of the Forty Days is the Christ who is reaching out to all who do not know Him, and who would be impatient with us if we were content to receive His blessing for ourselves alone. He sends us forth with His blessing, clothes us with His own authority, and gives us His very own name and power. The Lord helps us to be faithful to Him below as He faithfully represents us before His Father above.

Three Calls

And so these three appearances represent three calls. The first is His coming to the individual; the second, His coming to the little company; and the third, to the assembled congregation of believers. In the same way, He still comes to us alone, comes in our friendships and family circle, and comes in the assembly of His saints.

The first was His coming as a Friend, the second as a Teacher, the third as a Master to send forth His disciples to His work. And, finally, the first emphasizes the Christ Himself, the second His Word, and the third His Spirit.

And now, in conclusion, what does all this mean for us today? Not only, beloved, that these forty days may be prolonged for us until His coming again, but, perhaps, that in these last times they may be especially repeated as the precursors of His second coming. For as He gradually and slowly withdrew from earth, lingering those forty days from the cross to the throne, so gradually will He return; and before we see Him in the clouds, we will be conscious of a nearer presence on the earth below.

It is said that a Russian emperor used to visit all parts of his realm incognito, so that he might know his people and be able rightly to rule them. Would it be strange if the blessed Christ should even now be passing to and fro on this earth, on many a special inspection, before He erects His throne and calls His cabinet around Him from the men and women whom He has tried and proved? We know that as Nehemiah returned to Jerusalem, he went out alone and surveyed the ruined city, and then summoned his hosts to restore it. (See Nehemiah 2:11–18.) And so Christ, even today, in the dark night of the ages, is walking around Zion, surveying her bulwarks and her ruined towers, and preparing for her restoration in millennial glory. Oh, that we may know Him now and be with Him then, that we may not miss the Morning Star, and so be up in time to pass full-robed into the wedding feast with the risen Sun of Righteousness on that millennial day that is drawing nigh! Amen.

3

THE SECOND WEEK:
THE UNBELIEVING DISCIPLE

At the meeting on the first Sabbath evening in the upper room, one disciple was absent. *"Thomas,...called Didymus, was not with them when Jesus came"* (John 20:24). The disciples seem to have sought him during the days that followed, and they carried to him, in his discouragement and despondency, the joyful tidings of the Master's appearing. But his true and tender heart, just because it loved so much, was unable to take in the message that seemed too good to be true. And, with an obstinacy born not only of self-will and unbelief but also, perhaps, in some measure, of a love that would not dare to trust its hopes to anything less than absolute certainty, he declared, *"Except I shall see in his hands the print of the nails,...and thrust my hand into his side, I will not believe"* (John 20:25).

At length the week is past, and the following First Day evening finds them again assembled to talk about the one absorbing theme. Suddenly, as before, Jesus reveals Himself in their midst. Instantly approaching Thomas, He holds out to him His hands and opens His garment for him to thrust his fingers into His once-wounded side. The act is, doubtless, free from all severity or even suggestion of harshness and censoriousness. With tender condescension, He seems to entirely overlook the obstinate unreasonableness of the disciple and to be concerned only with removing his difficulties and helping him to believe, for He adds, *"Be not faithless, but believing"* (John 20:27).

But Thomas is overwhelmed not so much by the physical evidences presented to him as by the heart-searching omniscience of his Lord and the tender grace that has so submitted to his proud and unbelieving demands. Refusing, it would seem, to accept the proffered evidence, Thomas throws himself at his Master's feet with one adoring cry, *"My Lord and my God"* (John 20:28). And as Jesus beholds him, He adds with gentle reproof and yet benediction, *"Thomas, because thou hast seen me, thou hast believed: blessed are they that have not seen, and yet have believed"* (John 20:29).

What are the lessons of this beautiful scene for us, and how does the Lord still reproduce this incident of the forty days in our lives?

1. Christ Especially Recognizes and Honors the Sabbath Day

Jesus' appearance to Thomas and the other disciples reveals a Christ who especially recognizes and honors the Sabbath Day. True, it was not the Hebrew Sabbath but the first day of the week. Yet, advisedly, we call it the Sabbath, for it has undoubtedly taken the place of the hallowed Old Testament Sabbath, and surely that name is preferable to the heathen word *Sunday*, named after one of the gods of the Anglo-Saxons. Of course, "the Lord's Day" is the sweetest name, but we cannot always force it into the phraseology of current speech. And between the two names that usually denote the day, it is certainly preferable to use the Bible name where we cannot, without pedantry, employ the simpler "Lord's Day" of the New Testament.

Christ has undoubtedly taught us that He is Lord of the Sabbath day, and, as its Lord, He has adopted it and modified it by a change of time and by a change and elevation of its spirit and signification. There can be no doubt that among the instructions He gave to His disciples during the forty days, when we are told that He spoke to them *"of the things pertaining to the kingdom of God"* (Acts 1:3), the Lord revealed to them abundant reasons and gave them authoritative commands for the change of the day. Otherwise, their own practice would not have been changed, as we find that it was. So, for us, their conduct is conclusive of something behind it, namely, His own explicit injunctions.

We believe, therefore, that Jesus took the Old Testament Sabbath, which had come down through the ages and passed through Judaism—a temporary dispensation that, for a time, linked itself with the Sabbath that was much older—and incorporated it into the New Testament system, with the added significance of His resurrection and the appropriate change from the day that marked only the finishing of creation to that which expressed the beginning of the new creation, which the resurrection of Jesus had introduced. And, as He designed it to possess a special significance, He Himself observed it with the most sacred emphasis.

It is very impressive that Jesus should have held Himself from the presence of His brethren for an entire week, so that He might more emphatically mark His coming the second time on this day. All His previous appearances had been on the same day the previous week, and He allows the long interval of six days to pass, notwithstanding all their longing to behold Him again, and the affectionate interest of His own loving heart toward them. He did this so that He might come to them again on the First Day and signalize their meeting in the upper room as the foundation of the permanent worship of the future church.

Wise and happy are those who imitate their Lord in this way and separate this hallowed day from other days unto Him and His fellowship and service! The scrupulous observance of the Lord's Day will always be found to be a test of consistent Christian living and a source and channel of strength and grace throughout the week. The countries that have desecrated the Lord's Day are marked by irreligion, immorality, and national decline, and those that honor God's day are correspondingly blessed. Additionally, the individuals who hold this sacred day distinct from secular care and occupation will always find that it is the key to a happy, holy, and successful week, and that those who rob it of its rest and sacredness rob themselves and not the altar of their God.

Like the best room of our house, the Sabbath should be kept apart from the workbench and the implements and employments of our secular toil. As we would not bring the kitchen or the shop into the parlor, let us not take our bartering and bargaining, our secular cares and plans, our newspapers and our letter writing, and all the confusion and turmoil of the week into its inner chamber, which, like the ancient Holy of Holies, should be for the Lord alone and the choicest blessings of His presence and communion.

It is not the sanction of law that makes the Sabbath sacred but the higher law of love and blessing that Jesus has brought to it. It is the day we keep for Him, and we may be very sure it is the day that He keeps for us and the day in which He comes, above all others, to meet His own in His own sacred courts and in their secret closets. Let us remember, therefore, that the Christ of the Forty Days is still the Christ preeminently of the First Day. His presence and benediction will still overshadow, until the end of time, the Christian Sabbath and make it the Day of days.

2. Christ Comes on the Sabbath to Speak to Our Hearts, Consciences, and Experiences

The Christ of the Forty Days is One who comes on the Sabbath to speak to the very hearts and consciences and experiences of His disciples. He is One who knows what they have been doing, thinking, and saying throughout the week. He had missed Thomas on that former Sabbath evening and knew well what it was going to cost him. He had heard Thomas's willful words and unbelief during the week in answer to his brethren. Therefore, He shows him that He knows all his sin and doubt.

So, still, He meets us on this day and in His house. Have we not often wondered as we have felt our hearts unveiled and our inmost thoughts revealed by some message from His servant that seemed to show us all we ever did, and almost to be the echo of our own thoughts during the days that had passed before? Perhaps, we have instinctively felt that somebody has been reporting our words or our actions to the preacher. Perhaps, the very question that we have been asking and wishing somebody would answer comes back to us in the light of His Word, as spoken by one who did not know of our thoughts, and we wonder and adore, like Thomas, at the feet of Him whose Word

> is quick, and powerful, and sharper than any twoedged sword, piercing even to the dividing asunder of soul and

spirit, and of the joints and marrow, and is a discerner of the thoughts and intents of the heart. Neither is there any creature that is not manifest in his sight: but all things are naked and opened unto the eyes of him with whom we have to do.
(Hebrews 4:12–13)

Nor is this unveiling and revealing always accompanied by a sense of reproof and condemnation, for it is most comforting to know that we are in the presence of One who has already diagnosed our disease and laid His hand upon the sore, so that He might heal it. And we feel like adding, with the biblical writer, *"Let us therefore come boldly unto the throne of grace, that we may obtain mercy, and find grace to help in time of need"* (Hebrews 4:16).

It is very touching to notice how the Master immediately went to Thomas. The very first one whom He sought out was the one who was troubled and perplexed. And so, if your heart has a single care or questioning, it is to you that He is coming now with help and blessing. He has light for your perplexity, strength for your weakness, comfort for your sorrow, love for your loneliness, and supply for all your need. For His blessing is always in season and exactly suited to the very need of the present moment. Let us, therefore, bring Him even our darkest doubts, our deepest despondencies, our most unworthy thoughts, the things we naturally would seek to hide. For He knows everything already and has come to deliver us and to bring us grace and help in the time of need—that is, the very grace we need today.

Jesus has light for your perplexity, strength for your weakness, comfort for your sorrow, love for your loneliness, and supply for all your need.

3. Christ Has Infinite Patience and Tenderness Toward Doubters and Sinners

We learn from this story that the Christ of the Forty Days is a Christ of infinite patience and tenderness toward the doubting and even toward the sinning. How gentle His treatment of Thomas—how free from all upbraiding! How careful He was to avoid every irritation and offense and to withhold the gentle reproof that He afterward uttered until Thomas was restored! He even condescended to meet Thomas's imperious demand literally and fully, granting all that Thomas claimed. He knew it was not the highest kind of faith to give Thomas, but He gave him what he asked for and then told him how much better the higher faith would have been.

How gently He has led us all! How many times He has answered prayer in temporal things for us as the sign of His willingness to do greater things, and given us evidences of His love and care, to nurture our faith to higher ventures and achievements! How tenderly He has borne with us in our backslidings and our unbeliefs! How much He has done for our imperfect faith! How often He has forgiven our unworthy doubts, and, even when our faith failed, did not permit His faithfulness to fail, so leading us on gently until we had learned to trust Him in some measure worthy of His faithfulness, love, and power. If only we have an honest purpose, He will take our faith that is just as a grain of mustard seed and cherish it into maturity and do exceedingly abundantly above all its deserving.

Even the honest skeptic is not rejected from His mercy and is held insofar as he will follow the light that he already possesses. The prayer "God help me, if there is a God," if it is all the prayer the doubting can offer, will not be in vain, as has sometimes been strangely proved. The soul struggling from old traditions into the fullness of the gospel and slowly letting go of its limitations and prejudices should not be discouraged if it does not get everything into freedom immediately. The Master will take all that you can give and will lead you further if you will follow.

The suffering one who has caught a glimmer of the light of the healing power of the Great Physician should not fear that he will be rejected because he is struggling with doubts and fears. Only follow the light that is clear, and press on into all that is added, and "you will know, if you follow on to know the Lord." (See Hosea 6:3.) *"A bruised reed shall he not break, and the smoking flax shall he not quench"* (Isaiah 42:3); nor will He, amid all your fluctuations, "fail or be discouraged" with you till He has "brought forth judgment" into victory. (See Isaiah 42:3–4.) Blessed, patient Christ, how You have borne with us! How You have lifted us up when we were fallen, brought us back from our stumbling, and "established our goings"! (See Psalm 40:2.) Oh, help us to be more like You in our gentleness and patience with those who are out of the way.

4. The Revelation of Christ Is the Answer to All Our Doubts and Difficulties

This incident also teaches us that the true answer to all our doubts and difficulties is the revelation of Christ Himself. Jesus healed Thomas of his skepticism not by reasoning with him but by showing him Himself. He reached out and showed to him the marks from the nails, and He opened His bosom and said, in essence, "Reach hither your hand and thrust it into My side and feel, if you will, the very beating of My heart." (See John 20:27.) And Thomas needed no more. He had seen the Lord; he had felt His living flesh; and, above all, he had realized His heart-searching omniscience, and he was satisfied.

Once more, this is the answer to all our doubts and questionings. This is the answer God has given. For *"God, who at sundry times and in divers manners spake in time past unto the fathers by the prophets, hath in these last days spoken unto us by his Son"* (Hebrews 1:1–2). Jesus Christ is God's last Word to us. The skeptic is not going to be convinced by your reasoning but by God's Christ. Show him the Lord Jesus, the marvelous though simple story of His life, the vivid picture of His death, but, above all, the testimony of His resurrection and the revelation of His living presence and power today among His people as the unchanging Christ of the Forty Days, and he, too, will say, *"My Lord and my God"* (John 20:28).

Christ wants us to show Him to the world. Our argument is not our logic and theology but our Lord Himself. *"Ye shall be witnesses unto me"* (Acts 1:8). This is all Jesus needs, that we tell about Him and make Him real to others. This is also the solution to all the sinner's difficulties. You cannot save him by preaching theology to him. But show him Christ, his crucified, living, welcoming Savior, and all his doubts have fled.

This is the solution to all questions about sanctification. We may seek blessings and experiences, states and conditions, and find that we have to go over it all again and again. But let us only see Jesus *"who of God is made unto us wisdom, and righteousness, and sanctification, and redemption"* (1 Corinthians 1:30), and we are satisfied and go forth with the joyful cries, *"I live; yet not I, but Christ liveth in me"* (Galatians 2:20), and *"I can do all things through Christ which strengtheneth me"* (Philippians 4:13).

This is the solution to all questions about healing. It is not enough to know the theory and doctrine; we must behold the life and receive it from Him. Let us but see Jesus as our risen Lord and our living Head, and ourselves as *"members of his body, of his flesh, and of his bones"* (Ephesians 5:30), and our physical being will be baptized into His life and fullness and go forth with all-sufficient springs of heavenly life.

This is the answer to all our difficulties with circumstances in our work for Christ and our earthly trials. Let us but see the Master's hand in everything, and above all let us only behold the Captain marching upon the field, and, lo! our fears are gone, and we begin to shout, "Thanks be to God, who gives us the victory through our Lord Jesus Christ!" (See 2 Corinthians 2:14.)

Beloved, this Christ is standing by your side today, unrecognized for so long. He cries to you, *"Behold, I stand at the door, and knock: if any man hear my voice, and open the door, I will come in to him, and will sup with him, and he with me"* (Revelation 3:20). Look to Him—away from yourself, from your troubles, from your doubts, from your theories! It is a Person you need, and this Person is the Christ of the gospel, the Christ of the Forty Days, the Christ who *"is the same yesterday, today and forever"* (Hebrews 13:8 NKJV), and the Christ who is hovering over you now and waiting to possess your heart forever.

5. Christ Is Divine

"My Lord and My God" (John 20:28) was the testimony of the man who had doubted, and whose doubts were in one moment turned into a testimony that would be blasphemy if applied to anyone other than God. The expression *"Lord"* signifies the place of supreme control and government over all nature and providence; and the word *"God"* is expressive of the absoluteness of God in His divine nature as the external and supreme Creator and all-sufficient and almighty One.

Thomas recognizes the glorious presence before him as no less than the eternal God, the God of the Old Testament in all the majesty of His revealing, the God of nature and providence in all the glory of His power and dominion. Oh, it is much for us to fully realize that this is indeed the name and character of our Christ! This was what Peter meant that day when he stood before the proud Sanhedrin and declared that *"God hath made the same Jesus, whom ye have crucified, both **Lord** and **Christ"*** (Acts 2:36). In that hour, Peter saw Jesus as the supreme and majestic Lord of nature and of men, holding in His hand the very lives of the men before him, and having all power in heaven and in earth. It is one thing for us to say these words; it is another for us to realize, in our quickened consciousness in our inmost being, that we are talking to One and intimately linked with One who holds in His hand at this moment all events and destinies.

It is He of whom Isaiah said, *"All nations before him are as nothing....He taketh up the isles as a very little thing....The Creator of the ends of the earth, fainteth not, neither is weary...there is no searching of His understanding"* (Isaiah 40:17, 15, 28). Oh, beloved, is this Christ our Christ? Does He stand over against our difficulties and above our adversaries, and have we crowned Him *Lord* of all? The secret of this for us means that He has become our Lord and our God.

Jesus is the supreme Lord of nature and of men, having all power in heaven and in earth.

---

6. Christ Expects Our Implicit Faith

In this meeting, Jesus speaks of two kinds of faith. First, He says, "Thomas, you have seen and have believed." (See John 20:29.) He does not despise this faith but accepts it, such as it is, though He pronounces no high benediction on it. It is the faith that has sprung from sight and reached its conclusion from outward evidence.

But there is another aim—a higher faith. Upon this He pronounces an everlasting blessing as He looks into our faces in these coming ages, upon everyone who will meet this benediction: *"Blessed are they that have not seen, and yet have believed"* (John 20:29). Undoubtedly, He means that it would have been better for Thomas to have believed the testimony of his brethren, even before he saw his Lord. Then, indeed, he would have received a blessing that perhaps none of them had received. He had an opportunity, given perhaps to none other, of believing before he beheld a manifestation of Christ. All the others seemed to have beheld Him for themselves before they believed. Thomas might have believed on their word and had this mighty blessing, but he missed it, and it passed over to us in later times. Happy are those who have claimed it! Happy are we if we will always claim it, and, venturing out on the simple word of our God, will always dare to take Him by simple faith before we see the moving of His hand or the evidences of His power, and will even shout with the Hebrew prophet, *"Although the fig tree shall not blossom, neither shall fruit be in the vines...yet I will rejoice in the Lord, I will joy in the God of my salvation"* (Habakkuk 3:17–18).

Is there anyone reading these words who is yet unsaved? Beloved, the greatest blessing of your existence is before you! Will you take God at His Word and dare this moment to believe that as you go to Him in your unworthiness and helplessness, He does not cast you out but now receives you and saves you according to His Word? Blessed are you at this very moment! You have not seen—but you will see—the glory and the grace of God.

Is there anyone reading these words who has not believed His mighty promise of deliverance from sin and perfect keeping through His indwelling presence and Holy Spirit? Beloved, He bids you take Him this moment at His mighty Word, if you will but yield yourself and claim it: *"If we confess our sins, he is faithful and just to forgive us our sins, and to cleanse us from all unrighteousness"* (1 John 1:9). *"Now ye are clean through the word which I have spoken unto you"* (John 15:3). *"The blood of Jesus Christ [God's] Son cleanseth us from all sin"* (1 John 1:7). *"Come out from among them, and be ye separate,...and I will receive you....I will dwell in [you], and walk in [you]...and will be a Father unto you, and ye shall be my sons and daughters, saith the Lord Almighty"* (2 Corinthians 6:17, 16, 18). *"I will put my spirit within you, and cause you to walk in my statutes, and ye shall keep my judgments"* (Ezekiel 36:27).

Will you believe these promises right now without waiting for some internal evidences or some manifested fruit in your life? Will you dare to believe that God becomes these things to you this very hour and until your lifework is done? Will you press forward and *"hold fast the profession of* [your faith] *without wavering"* (Hebrews 10:23)? Blessed are you, for you have not seen and yet have believed, and already He is about to answer your trust by the witnessing voice of His Holy Spirit and the joy of His full salvation.

Is there anyone reading these words who has longed to feel the power of His touch in his body, who has been waiting for some external sign or manifestation before fully resting and abandoning himself to His power? Beloved, will you not venture to trust Him who *"Himself took our infirmities, and bare our sicknesses"* (Matthew 8:17)? Is this not enough? Will you not roll them on Him this very hour?

"The prayer of faith shall save the sick" (James 5:15). Will you not spring to meet this promise and dare to believe that the Lord does raise you up? *"When ye pray, believe that ye receive them* [the

things for which you ask]" (Mark 11:24). Will you so receive? Blessed are you already, trusting one! You are blessed far more in the trusting than in the answer that is coming, surely coming, for that is not the blessing. The blessing is not that He is going to give you what you trusted Him for, but it is that He can trust you, that He can take you into the place of His confidential ones and rejoice in you as one who can trust your God without reserve, and to whom He can confide the banner of His conflict and His testimony before the world.

Is there anyone reading these lines who has long been wondering why his prayers have not been answered, and who has been waiting for some evidence of the providence of God? Beloved, God has delayed the evidence to give you the opportunity for your greatest blessings. He wants you to be one of the heroes of faith who will stand in the forlorn hope and at the front line of the battle, following at your Leader's command, although no other soldier may stand by your side and no way may seem possible through those ranks and foes. May God help you not to miss your opportunity and your garland of victory! Press out to meet your Captain. *"Said I not unto thee,"* Jesus cries, *"that, if thou wouldest believe, thou shouldest see the glory of God?"* (John 11:40). Lift up this very moment the hands that hang down and strengthen the feeble knees! (See Isaiah 35:3; Hebrews 12:12.) *"Believe in the LORD your God, so shall ye be established; believe his prophets, so shall ye prosper"* (2 Chronicles 20:20). Send forth the choirs of praise to the front line of the battle. Claim your answer and declare your victory, and already your own heart will feel the march of the Conqueror and His benediction upon your head. *"Blessed are they that have not seen, and yet have believed"* (John 20:29).

This power to believe God when we have nothing but God to believe is itself blessing. It is said of Abraham that he was like

Him whom he believed, who *"calleth those things which be not as though they were"* (Romans 4:17). Faith is a kind of Godlikeness.

Let us not miss our opportunity and God's expectation of us! Has He not a right, after all His patience, love, power, and revealing of Himself to us, to expect our perfect trust? And will He not have it henceforth from all our hearts, in all our ways?

4

THE LORD'S MESSAGE TO THE UNBELIEVING CHURCH

"Afterward [Jesus] appeared unto the eleven as they sat at meat, and upbraided them with their unbelief and hardness of heart, because they believed not them which had seen him after he was risen. And he said unto them, Go ye into all the world, and preach the gospel to every creature. He that believeth and is baptized shall be saved; but he that believeth not shall be damned."
—Mark 16:14–16

The meeting described above was probably the sequel to the incident in connection with the restoration of Thomas. It could not have occurred on the first Sabbath of the resurrection, because we are told here that Jesus *appeared unto the eleven as they sat at meat,* and there were not eleven disciples at the first interview. Thomas was absent. Even so, it was an early meeting after the resurrection; and, undoubtedly, it seems to have been the one involving Thomas, the first part of which we have already discussed.

The sentence with which the meeting is introduced in the gospel of Mark, respecting Jesus' upbraiding of the disciples for their hardness of heart and unbelief because they did not believe those to whom He had appeared after His resurrection, seems very significantly to apply to Thomas and what the Lord said to him at that time. The following words are probably the concluding messages of the meeting, as, turning from Thomas to the other ten, Jesus gave them this Great Commission and the credentials of His power, saying,

> *Go ye into all the world, and preach the gospel to every creature. He that believeth and is baptized shall be saved; but he that believeth not shall be damned. And these signs shall follow them that believe; in my name shall they cast out devils; they shall speak with new tongues; they shall take up serpents; and if they drink any deadly thing, it shall not hurt them; they shall lay hands on the sick, and they shall recover.* (Mark 16:15–18)

This is Jesus' message to the church under the Christian dispensation. It must be in force until the entire world is evangelized, and it must be taken together and not piecemeal. As long as the command to preach the gospel to every creature is in force, so long must the promises of Christ's cooperating and supernatural power also be regarded as operative. And yet, the attitude of the church has been one of chronic unbelief in regard to this matter, an unbelief in the promises equaled only by tardiness in obeying the command. However, as the church springs to meet the latter, she seems to be recovering and regaining her faith in the former. And it is indeed remarkable that the revival of the missionary spirit in our day is marked by the restoration of the supernatural gifts of the apostolic age.

The unbelief of Christ's church in these things seems to be almost hinted at in the way the passage is introduced. It begins with the account of His upbraiding the eleven for their unbelief. And their spirit would seem to have been typical of the sin that so easily was to beset the ages that were to follow. May the Lord help us to rise out of this paralyzing influence and to fully understand and enter into the meaning and the power of these mighty words, which He has left to us to the end of time as His Great Commission!

1. The Gospel Is Glad Tidings for Those Who Believe

From this meeting of Jesus with His disciples, we learn the nature and conditions of the gospel. The word *gospel*, of course, means the glad tidings of salvation, through the finished work of Jesus Christ, to the entire world and to all the ages, insofar as those who hear the gospel are willing to meet its simple conditions.

It is, indeed, glad tidings. It tells rebellious men that God is reconciled; that justice is satisfied; that sin has been atoned for; that the judgment of the guilty may be revoked, the condemnation of the sinner cancelled, the curse of the law blotted out, the gates of hell closed, the portals of heaven opened wide, the power of sin subdued, the guilty conscience healed, the broken heart comforted, the sorrow and misery of the fall undone, the very king of terrors himself destroyed, and all the evils and miseries of ruined humanity completely overcome and transformed into blessings more glorious and lasting than Adam ever lost or unfallen man could ever have enjoyed.

And the condition of all this blessing is stated in the simplest terms. There is no restriction in the terms, for the message is addressed to *"every creature"* (Mark 16:15). The only condition is, *"He that believeth and is baptized shall be saved; but he that believeth not shall be damned"* (Mark 16:16). It is evident, therefore, that the rite of baptism is not a condition for salvation; its omission will not bring condemnation, though its acceptance is commanded wherever it is possible. The one essential condition, therefore, is simply believing; that is, believing the "glad tidings."

This is not spoken of as some abstruse and unattainable experience but the simple, frank acceptance of the glad tidings as true and as our own. It is, in a word, to believe the facts respecting Jesus Christ and His finished work and to accept and appropriate the salvation for ourselves, to simply believe that it becomes our own by virtue of our accepting it. The logical process is as simple as the alphabet. Christ offers salvation to me, and I heartily accept it; therefore, I have it because I accept it, and because God has promised it to all who will accept it.

There is no mystery about this, no strain. It is as plain as the untutored faith of the little newsboy who, lying on a heap of filthy straw, had caught a glimpse of the gospel in a street meeting and, in his dying moments, had sent for a missionary to ask him, "Missionary, is it true as how you said that Jesus Christ would save any feller who ax'd him?" "Yes," said the missionary, "it is true; He says so." "Then," said the little fellow as he clasped his dying hands and looked into heaven with a face already shining with the heavenly light, "He saves me, 'cos I axes Him."

That is the gospel in its simplicity and its profundity—simply believing the glad tidings and taking the benefit to ourselves without doubt or questioning. That was the answer Paul had one night for the jailer at Philippi: *"Believe on the Lord Jesus Christ, and thou shalt be saved"* (Acts 16:31). That is the message that the minds of heathendom can always understand, and that only those whose self-sufficiency and earthly wisdom are looking for something higher and harder will miss. It is the gospel for the masses, the gospel for the heathen, the gospel for children, the gospel for the whole creation. Oh, that we might send it forth, that there might be no son or daughter of Adam's race who has not heard the glorious tidings, which are so free to all and so easy for everyone to receive!

The gospel in its simplicity and its profundity is simply to believe the glad tidings and to take the benefit to ourselves without doubt or questioning.

To *"He that believeth,"* Jesus adds, *"and is baptized"* (Mark 16:16). We cannot divorce baptism from believing, nor should we divorce the believing from the baptism. Again, it is a great mistake to make baptism a gospel or a theology that can in any measure detract from the prominence of Christ and the simplicity of faith. Yet, to every heart that truly accepts the gospel, it is a sacred obligation and delightful privilege to make full acknowledgement of our Master and Lord in God's appointed way and thus, like Him, to *"fulfil all righteousness"* (Matthew 3:15).

And to those who have learned the deeper and sweeter meaning of the ordinance itself as the special symbol of death and resurrection with Christ, it is a joy unspeakable to enter with Him into the death of self and sin and to rise into the fullness of the resurrection life. But when we have said this, we have said all. The absence of baptism did not bar the dying thief from the courts of paradise (see Luke 23:39–43), nor will it bring the loss of salvation, under this precious verse, to any believing heart. And those who make baptism a means of regeneration, a condition of salvation, or a rigid term of Christian fellowship go further than the Lord Jesus intended here or than the apostle Paul tolerated for a moment when he said, *"Christ sent me not to baptize, but to preach the gospel"* (1 Corinthians 1:17). Baptism is not the gospel, although it is a most blessed symbol and seal of its reality and fullness.

2. Jesus' Followers Are Trustees of the Gospel

Christ has made His people trustees of the gospel for the world. He never meant that we should keep it as a selfish luxury, but that we should receive it and pass it on as a sacred trust for our entire sinful race. Instead of making us the trustees of the gospel, He might have sent the glad tidings to the world by some other means. Every angel in heaven would have been glad to bear such a message and would have counted it a high honor and divine joy to do so. But Christ has given this privilege to redeemed men; and, in a great measure, He has limited its diffusion by the human instrumentalities that spread it.

How disappointed and grieved His heart must be to see this precious trust withheld from those for whom He designed it and instead consumed for the selfish advantage of a few! Suppose a great benefactor gave a million dollars to relieve the poor of his city, placing the money in the hands of certain trustees. How would he feel if he found that those trustees were spending it for the support and enjoyment of themselves and their families and friends, and that the hundreds of poor children for whom it was intended were getting no benefit from his generous gift?

Such has literally been the attitude of the church of Christ for most of the centuries of the Christian age. It seems appalling when we stop to realize it! But, in giving the Great Commission, Christ does not allow the responsibility to be easily shifted off upon the abstract idea of the church, for it is a personal responsibility with each of the eleven disciples, and it has been transferred from them to every other disciple personally; and it is to continue being transferred in the same way until the end of the age.

Jesus' word was a distinct and individual message that necessarily implied the disciples' individual action. It was the command that scattered them, one by one, into all the world and sent them forth unto every creature. And the same command still rests upon every follower of Jesus, up to the utmost measure of his ability to fulfill it.

In this view of it, the Great Commission is a very simple responsibility but also a very great and serious one for which we are accountable. Looking in the face of every one of us, the Master asks, "Are you going to do what I tell you or not?" There is no possibility of evasion. He simply says, "Go ye" (Mark 16:15), and we must go or disobey. We believe, therefore, that every individual Christian is bound to his very utmost to spread the gospel, and to go personally if he can, without absolutely neglecting obligations at home that are imperative and that he can take as an excuse to the throne of God.

3. The Great Commission Is to the Whole World and the Whole Creation

The extent of this commission is to the whole world and the whole creation. All national restrictions are swept away by the broad and universal scope of redeeming mercy. Every race and country is included in the heart of God and the blood of Calvary; not only so, but also every creature. This includes far more than every man and woman. The word translated *"creature"* (Mark 16:15) means "creation," and it certainly includes the material and lower orders of creation.

"What!" you may ask, "are we to preach the gospel to the beast of the field, to the forests, to the wilderness, and to the mountains?" Yes, in the sense that there is nothing on earth, animate or inanimate, that is not going to benefit from the spreading of the gospel and the coming of the kingdom of Christ. That is what Jesus means. The whole material universe is to be made free through its uplifting power.

How the gospel has civilized the nations! How it is to drive away barbarism, cruelty, malaria and other diseases, barrenness, and, at last, death itself, from the whole creation that *"groaneth and travaileth in pain together until now,"* waiting for the time when *"the* [creation] *itself also shall be delivered from the bondage of corruption into the glorious liberty of the children of God"* (Romans 8:22, 21)!

Nowhere in the New Testament are we told that the whole world will accept the gospel, but we are told that the whole world will have the gospel preached to them. (See, for example, Matthew 24:14.) Christ's purpose will never be fulfilled until all the tribes are evangelized and have had the opportunity of accepting or rejecting the great salvation. As yet, a thousand millions of our race have not had the opportunity. And one hundred thousand every day are passing into eternity, to know their Savior and their God for the first time, and to cry, as they meet Him, "No man cared for my soul."

As you read every word of this sentence, a sad and sinful human spirit is passing into the presence of the Savior. That poor sad spirit is now looking down upon you and finding to his amazement that Christ died for his salvation, and that you knew this salvation and might have helped him to know it, too. What must Christ think of you as He turns, this moment, from that poor, shrinking, astonished soul to listen to your prayers, and then the next moment beholds another soul come with the same sad cry? One would think that He must almost lose heart in the prayers of His people and in the tender ministries of His love to us, when He knows that our brethren are perishing through our indolence and neglect.

It is useless for us to lay the matter over upon His omnipotence and say that He has power to save them in some other way. If there had been some other way of attaining the same results, then, surely, He went to needless expense in preparing the costly machinery of the cross and the gospel. It is very certain that God never would have sent His Son to die if salvation could have been obtained in any other way.

Doubtless, everything that tenderness and mercy can do to alleviate and modify the unspeakable loss and misery of ruined men will be done, for *"he that knew not, and did commit things worthy of stripes, shall be beaten with few stripes"* (Luke 12:48), but to be beaten with few stripes is far less than to be redeemed, cleansed, and made fitting to be partakers of the nature of God and the glory of heaven. To stand outside those gates is hell enough to one who has looked within them, and we know that without a new heart and the blood of Jesus, no member of the human race can ever enter heaven and share the prospects of God's redeemed. Whatever else awaits these myriads, it is not our salvation. Alas! alas! we know too well that most of them have sinned against the light of nature and have passed out of this mortal life with the consciousness already of unpardoned sin and the *"fearful looking for of judgment"* (Hebrews 10:27).

Oh, beloved, let us awake from all our dreams; and, for the sake of human pity and heavenly love, let us do what can be done to meet the simple, solemn, honest, imperative, irresistible command of Him who would not have spoken it if weaker speech could have sufficed.

The practicability of obeying this command makes the duty more binding. Dr. Hudson Taylor has shown that, in five years, every human being in China can be evangelized by sending merely one thousand missionaries to that country. And if this is so, two thousand more would reach all other races beneath the sun who have not yet heard the gospel. To do this, and to support them for one year, would cost only three million dollars, and this amount would be less than the fortune of many a Christian in this country. And to do it for five years would take only six million more; that is nine million altogether in the next five years, or less than two million a year. A smaller sum than the pettiest state in Europe could easily spend in some trivial war would be enough to accomplish the most majestic campaign that the universe has ever witnessed.

May God help each of us to understand the thought of our Captain, our ascended Christ, and to meet it faithfully and gloriously before this century shall close!

4. The Great Commission Is Accompanied by Majestic Credentials

The Great Commission is accompanied by majestic credentials—credentials worthy of so great a calling. Sending forth His ambassadors, the mighty, anointed King gives to each His signet ring and declares that the signs of His power will attend their ministry if they will only fulfill the simple condition of that power:

> *These signs shall follow them that believe; In my name shall they cast out devils; they shall speak with new tongues; they*

*shall take up serpents; and if they drink any deadly thing, it
shall not hurt them; they shall lay hands on the sick, and they
shall recover.*   (Mark 16:17–18)

The source of this supernatural power is found in the
phrase *"In my name"* (Mark 16:17). They were to recognize
themselves as representing Christ; they were to stand as men
with a Person behind them who was unseen to the world
except through His supernatural operation through their
words. They were to be His representatives; He was to be
their power. They were to be the hands on the dial, and He
the force behind it. They were to recognize themselves thus;
they were to introduce themselves to the world thus. They
were always to put Christ in front and stand behind Him, and
then expect to see Him work. *"In my name"* was the watch-
word of all this power.

Yet how different it has been! The church has a name, and
frequently it is not the name of Christ at all but of some human
founder or of some doctrinal phase. For example, believers go
out to meet the world and the devil in the name of a Wesley or an
episcopate or a presbytery; or a doctrine of baptism or a method
of Methodism. True, these are Christ's churches, but the very
principle on which their distinctiveness is founded obscures His
name. Frequently, the minister has a name so great that it quite
obscures the name of his Lord and renders it quite unnecessary.
The minister is known for his learning, for his eloquence, or his
influence more than for the supernatural power that follows
close behind him and accomplishes his ministry. Such workers cannot expect "these signs to follow in His name." We must
recognize ourselves as but figureheads, and all the power in the
unseen Presence that follows behind us and presses us forward as
the expression of its working.

Believers were to be Jesus' representatives;
He was to be their power.

Again, the forms in which this power was to be manifested are specifically expressed. The casting out of demons was to be one. Doubtless, this was meant to be the very same ministry that Christ had exercised for the deliverance of those possessed by evil spirits, a form of affliction that has existed in all ages and countries, and that still, undoubtedly, is the cause to which may be traced a great multitude of morbid mental conditions and forms of insanity.

This power was frequently exercised in the ministry of the apostles and became a testimony of great weight before the heathen world. It was the most impressive form of Paul's work, both in Philippi and in Ephesus. It has been marvelously revived in these last days and has been particularly prominent in the work of the mission field, especially in China. Of course, all that we have seen of the manifestation of Christ's power has been but fragmentary compared with what we might expect if the whole body of His church were united in faith and fellowship in the power of the Holy Spirit.

The gift of tongues was also promised and marvelously realized in the apostolic church, although this form of spiritual and supernatural influence was more abused than any other and less practical in its effectiveness. It seems to have been, in large measure, withdrawn at an early period. The promises of protection when "taking up serpents" and "drinking any deadly thing" seem to refer to the power to resist the element of poison where it comes from living or inorganic sources. These promises have often been fulfilled in the protection of God's servants from wild beasts and reptiles, the counteracting of otherwise fatal stings

from venomous creatures, and especially the influence of malig-
nant contagious diseases and unwholesome air and climatic
surroundings.

Of all these forms of supernatural power, the most prominent—because it is that which seems to have the most practical application and to be especially manifest in the facts that are
occurring in the church today—is the healing of the sick in the
name of Jesus. There is no doubt that this was regarded by the
Lord as supernatural healing, and that the laying on of hands
was designed as a symbolic act expressing His touch of power.
The fact that healing was promised is established by many other
Scripture passages; and the evidence of its fulfillment is found in
the whole apostolic history, the allusions in the epistles, the story
of the first four centuries of church history, and the records of the
past two hundred years in Protestant Christendom, especially
of the last twenty-five. Such healings are not always miraculous,
although the design of those referred to in Mark 16:18 is of this
character.

There seems to be a double provision for healing: one distinctly miraculous and the other the more ordinary working
of the divine life and power in the believing disciple. All these
manifestations mentioned in the book of Mark are called *"signs"*
(Mark 16:17) and are intended to be emphatic evidences to the
world of the presence and power of Christ and the reality of
His name. They are referred to later in the closing words of the
gospel: *"...the Lord working with them, and confirming the word
with signs following"* (Mark 16:20).

Henry Alford, Dean of Canterbury, in commenting on this
passage, declared that the promise of supernatural power was
not intended to be limited to the first age of the church; should
the occasion arise at any future time for the need of such manifestations, they may be reasonably expected in accordance with

this promise. However, the good dean neutralized his valuable admission by saying, "Where the gospel has been preached, as it has been in Christian countries, [these signs] are not needed now to establish the evidences of Christianity; and in heathen countries where the power of Christian nations extends, they are not needed because of these nations."

This is certainly a very weak admission. In the most advanced Christian nations, there is a deep need today for a real faith in something supernatural, especially in a religion that involves supernatural elements. Faith is becoming a sort of reasoning, and the Christian life a baptized morality and benevolent activity, but the expectation of anything actually supernatural, either in the hearts or bodies of men, is tabooed as fanaticism. Therefore, Christ has spoken out in the heart of Christian nations by the exhibitions of His miraculous power, even in these last days.

And as for the influence of Christian nations in heathen countries, the very name of *Christian* in China and Japan has usually been associated with the people who introduce licentiousness and rum, and whose morality is lower than heathenism. There is, indeed, a mighty need for the old credentials of the gospel. And if Christ can find the faith He is seeking (see, for example, Luke 18:8), He is as ready as ever to manifest His power.

5

THE THIRD WEEK: THE SCENE ON THE SHORES OF TIBERIAS

"This is now the third time that Jesus showed Himself to his disciples, after that he was risen from the dead."
—John 21:14

The above verse makes it certain that the incident recorded in John 21:1–23 follows the scenes in the preceding chapters from which we have just turned. It was probably the third week after the resurrection. During the previous week, the disciples had gone up to Galilee, according to Jesus' prior command and appointment (see Matthew 28:10, 16), having waited in Jerusalem only the one week after His resurrection in order that Thomas might be restored from his unbelief. They had doubtless returned to their former home, and they expected to meet their

Lord soon according to His appointment. But it would seem He did not come, and, as the days passed by, their means of livelihood perhaps having failed them, for these were poor men, their faith and hope began to fade and their prospects to grow dark and discouraging.

Then, the impetuous Simon proposed to several of their number to return to his former calling, at least for a time. And, getting into his little fishing boat with six of his brethren, he cast the net into the sea and waited for the reward of his toil. All night long they stayed at their posts and perhaps battled with the waves of the stormy little sea, till their hearts grew weary and faint as they found that their labor was in vain. And as the cold gray dawn slowly crept over the earth, their nets were empty still.

At that moment, they dimly saw a human form upon the shore, and a voice spoke to them in ordinary tones, *"Children, have ye any meat? They answered him, No"* (John 21:5). *"Cast the net on the right side of the ship,"* was the somewhat startling but quiet response, *"and ye shall find"* (John 21:6). Perhaps without fully realizing the right of the speaker to give such a command, they immediately obeyed. No sooner had they done so than their nets were filled with fish. The quick heart of John at once recognized the Lord. As soon as Peter heard that it was Christ, he swam to the shore and then drew the net to land, filled with large fish—one hundred fifty-three. (See John 21:11.)

The Lord tenderly prepared the morning meal, of which they were in such sore need, and He bade them bring the fish that they had caught and partake of the food that He had already prepared for them. As soon as their hunger was satisfied, He turned to Simon Peter and repeated the threefold question, *"Lovest thou me?"* (John 21:15, 16, 17) with such delicate allusion to Simon's fall (see, for example, Matthew 26:69–75), and such tender forgiving and restoring graciousness, that it seemed less like a reproof than a renewal of His commission and a call to higher service than he had ever dreamed of. With one added reproof in answer to Peter's impetuous and almost presumptuous question (see John 21:20–21), and one gentle hint with regard to the disciple whom Jesus loved[4] (see John 21:22–23), the scene closes, and the Master vanishes from their presence and our view, leaving this wondrous incident and its heart-searching lessons imprinted upon our hearts forever.

1. Christ Delivers Us and Reveals Himself to Us

The first lesson this meeting teaches us is that the Christ of the Forty Days comes to deliver us when we are baffled and perplexed and to reveal Himself as our Wonderful Counselor and Mighty God. (See Isaiah 9:6.) Perhaps, like Jesus' disciples, we have gone back a little to our own way and our old life, and the business has not prospered, the enterprise has not been successful, the painful struggle has been followed only by disappointment and the most trying extremities and even disasters. God may let the sinful world succeed in their forbidden schemes, but, blessed be His name, He does not allow His chosen ones to prosper in the path that leads them out of His holy will. He has a storm to send after every Jonah and an empty net for every unbelieving and inconstant Simon.

But in their failure, He does not fail. When they reach *"their wit's end"* and are ready to *"reel…and stagger like a drunken man"* (Psalm 107:27), then *"they cry unto the LORD in their trouble, and he saveth them out of their distresses"* (Psalm 107:19). How cheering it is to read about Paul telling the discouraged crew of the ship that their troubles have all come upon them because they

---

4. John. See, for example, John 21:7.

would not hear his counsel, but then adding the promise of the mercy and deliverance of God. (See Acts 27.)

Is there anyone reading these lines who has been passing through such a night of baffling struggles? Stop and think, dear friend, if perhaps you have gotten out of the will of your Father. Can you recall some command that summoned you to His work in another pathway of obedience, but you followed your own inclination and wisdom, so that you have been allowed to fail in order to bring you back like a lost sheep to His way? Only acknowledge your error and be willing to return, and lo! already He is standing at the shore to bring you out of your extremity and to place your feet upon the rock and establish your goings. (See Psalm 40:2.) Listen to the call of His providence and answer back, "*I will hear what God the* Lord *will speak: for he will speak peace unto His people, and to his saints: but let them not turn again to folly*" (Psalm 85:8).

Sometimes, however, without any conscious disobedience or willful departing from His path, we all have such nights of struggling and disappointment. Everything seems to fail us. We acted with our best judgment, and yet it came to nothing. We waited patiently, but there was no change for the better. And the heart at last grows sick with suspense and stagnation, and God seems to have forgotten to be gracious. Perhaps, we are in extreme circumstances, such as unemployed and without means, pressed on every side by difficulties and embarrassments, and seeing no way of escape, so that we can truly say, "O Lord, '*we have no might against this great company…; neither know we what to do: but our eyes are upon thee*'" (2 Chronicles 20:12).

Often, God allows His children to come into these straits so that He may work for them His greatest deliverances. And often He lets the trial linger to the very last degree of pressure and extremity—but He has not forgotten. All the night He has been watching and walking on that wave-beaten shore. Every sigh that the wind has borne across the sea has troubled His heart. Every pang of perplexity and suffering has found a sympathetic chord in His breast. He is only waiting until the night has run its course, the lesson has been fully learned, and the deliverance is ripe.

Often, God allows His children to experience difficulties so that He may work for them His greatest deliverances.

Even now, perplexed one, He is standing on the shore of your troubled sea. His form may be a very simple one, and you may not recognize your Lord in the ordinary-looking man before you or the commonplace circumstances coming to you, but *"it is the Lord"* (John 21:7)! He has come to show you what to do and say. *"Cast the net on the right side...and ye shall find"* (John 21:6). He is the Wonderful Counselor. He knows all the lines of influence, all the causes and effects in the realm of providence, and just where to bid you step and how to have you act so as to bring the result you require. *"There is no searching of his understanding"* (Isaiah 40:28). "Counsel is His and sound judgment. He leads in right paths and causes those who love Him to inherit substance, and He will fill their treasuries." (See Proverbs 8:14, 20–21.) Happy is the person of business who follows His wise counsels! Happy is the young person who makes Him the guide of his youth! Happy is the soul who trusts Him with all his heart and leans not on his own understanding! (See Proverbs 3:5.) Let us trust His wisdom, await His bidding, and follow His direction, no matter how all our experience may have contradicted it, and we will find that it will bring us to the desired end.

But He is also the Mighty God. Not only does He know on which side of the ship to cast the net, but He can also command the fish of the sea and fill that net with shoals in a moment. Every creature on the earth and in the sea is subject to His bidding, and every human heart is in His hand. He can change the counsels of men at His pleasure.

He gave Daniel favor with the king of Babylon and Joseph honor in Pharaoh's house. He can make men to be at peace with us and become the instruments of His will concerning us. He can send a little spider to weave its web over the mouth of the cave where the old Covenanter[5] is hidden from his pursuers and lead them to conclude, when they come on his track, "He has not entered there, because that spider's web is unbroken and undisturbed." He can send a hen to lay a single egg every morning where Alexander Peden[6] is hiding, and furnish the saint with his breakfast without a suspicion from his foes. He can bid the ravens feed Elijah, the bees wait on John the Baptist, the quails come to the table of Israel's hosts, and the scorpions refuse to sting or harm the faithful missionary. He can prosper the honorable and consecrated merchant, regulate the markets of the world, and consecrate the gain of men to Himself at His own mighty will.

> He every where hath sway,
> And all things serve his might.
>
> . . . .
>
> Leave to his Sovereign sway
> To choose and to command;
> With wonder fill'd, thou then shalt own
> How wise, how strong his hand.[7]

---

5. A Covenanter was a member of the Scottish Presbyterian movement of the seventeenth century.
6. A prominent leader in the Covenanter movement.
7. Isaac Watts and John Rippon, *Dr. Watts' Psalms and Hymns with Dr. Rippon's Selection* (London: William Wittemore, and Holston and Stoneman, 1840), #306.

2. Our Temporal Deliverances Are Intended to Lead Us to Higher Spiritual Blessing and Service

This wonderful miracle of fish was an occasion for something far more than the mere help it brought the disciples at a time of perplexity and distress. It was, in fact, a type of the new life and work into which Jesus was leading them. It was the second catch of fish that He had miraculously given them. The first, three years earlier, had called them to the first stage of their apostolic ministry. But that first stage had been a comparative failure— something like the first catch of fish; for then, it will be remembered, their nets broke and the miracle ended in confusion. And so ended the first three years of their service, in the wretched failure of the crucifixion days, well near the entire abandonment of their new hopes and confidences.

But the second catch of fish was entirely different from the first. These were all large fish, and they were all brought safely to land. Such was to be the disciples' future ministry as *"fishers of men"* (Matthew 4:19; Mark 1:17). The souls they were to bring to Christ were to be such souls, and their fruit was to remain and to grow a hundredfold until it filled the world and the heaven above. Henceforth, they were to fish with the Master on the shore, casting their net always on the right side of the ship at His constant bidding. His wisdom and power were to attend their labors and make the miracle of that Galilean shore perpetual in the years and centuries that were to follow.

And so, when He comes to us in His mighty providences, delivering us out of our distresses and manifesting His infinite wisdom and power, it means much more than the temporal deliverance. God intends it as a type of our future and a pledge of His wisdom and power for all our coming needs, and He is almost always calling us to learn some deeper spiritual lesson, to reach out to some higher experience, and to go forth to some larger service for Him. Behind our temporal trials and providential blessings there always may be traced a spiritual meaning, and out of them often come our richest blessings. God loves to take the most commonplace thing and transform it by giving it a heavenly meaning.

For example, He took Jacob's trial that night at Peniel and turned it into the crisis of his life, sending him forth the next morning with the new name of Israel, to be the head of the future tribes that bear that name. (See Genesis 32:1–30.) Saul, when searching for his lost donkeys, found not only the donkeys but a kingdom, too, and went home from the prophet's house another man, to enter a higher sphere and service. (See 1 Samuel 9–10.) David's rescue of his lambs from the lion and the bear became the token and pledge of his being entrusted as the shepherd of God's flock and the captain of God's army. (See 1 Samuel 17:17–58.)

Therefore, beloved, as you read these lines, if you recognize in your life the intervention of your Father's hand and your Master's love and power, remember that your blessing is lost if it terminates upon itself, and that God is calling you through it to a higher service and a nobler place than you have ever known. Arise and meet Him. Understand the meaning of His visitation. Do not miss the blessing of His coming into your life but go forth from this hour to recognize your higher calling and to understand the Presence that has given you the pledge of His own all-sufficient might for everything that His higher service can henceforth require at your hands.

Has He healed your body? It is so that the life restored may be glorious for Him. Has He delivered you out of financial difficulties? Remember that your business is henceforth His and a sacred trust for Him. Has He marvelously answered prayer? Remember that He has given you the key to the mercy seat and called you henceforth to a ministry of prayer for others and for Him. May God help you to realize your blessing as a trust and consecrate it to His highest will and the glory of His name!

3. Christ Comes to Us to Feed Our Souls and Supply Our Spiritual Need

Jesus comes to us, just as He went to His disciples, not only to deliver us from our trials and to call us to higher service but also to feed our souls with heavenly bread and supply all our spiritual need. *"Come and dine"* (John 21:12) is His word to us as well as to them. Mere answered prayer is not sufficient for the soul's hunger, nor even Christian work in its most successful forms. Amid outward prosperity and abounding activity, the soul may be starving—and often is—and men and women break down in the Lord's work because they give out more than they replenish. They have not learned the secret of this simple call: *"Come and dine."*

"I believe the secret of my frequent attacks of nervousness and physical suffering," said a friend the other day, "is that I am doing too much work for the Lord and taking too little time for communion with Him." This friend was probably right. God often has to knock a little rudely at the door of our sensitive nerves to call us to the hour of communion and to the "dining room" where He renews our spiritual strength. The bread and the fish were brought by Him, and the meal was prepared by His own hands. And so Christ Himself must feed us with His living bread by that spiritual process that only He can make plain and real.

Amid outward prosperity and abounding activity,
the soul may be starving. It has not learned the secret
of Christ's simple call, "Come and dine."

But the disciples, too, had something to do. Jesus told them, *"Bring of the fish which ye have now caught"* (John 21:10). Why was this? Oh, the Lord wants us to minister to Him, as well as to receive from Him, and our service finds its true end when it becomes food for our dear Lord. He was pleased to feed on their fish while they were feeding on His. It was the double banquet of which He speaks in the tender message of Revelation: *"I...will sup with him, and he with me"* (Revelation 3:20). Beloved, are we feeding upon our Lord, and are we ministering to our Lord? Then, indeed, is the ancient peace offering truly fulfilled in our blessed fellowship with Jesus, and our service truly consecrated when it ministers to His joy and glory.

4. Christ Comes to Restore Us from Our Failures and to Call Us to Nobler Services

In addition, the Christ of the Forty Days still comes to restore us from our failures and to turn them to blessed account by calling us to nobler services just because of them. The exquisite scene with Simon Peter does not need to be analyzed here in detail, further than to say that those three questions, *"Lovest thou me?"* (John 21:15, 16, 17), were not all the same. There was a shade of difference in each, and a cumulative force in all, that brought back most distinctly to Peter's conscience the memory of his three denials of Jesus, and the cause of those denials in his own self-confidence and vainglorious strength.

In the same way, the Master comes to us to recall the memory of our faults and failures so keenly that we will not miss the lesson, but so delicately that we will not be wounded by the recollection. And then, so completely does He forgive and forget that we know that all the fault has been undone forever and all the failure more than restored by His grace and love.

There is always something for us to learn out of situations like those the disciples experienced. Beloved, the trials through which we have been passing have been intended to show something imperfect in you and me, something in our life that the Master wants different. He does not want to depress or discourage us. He wishes simply to hint at the defect and then to have us rise above it and forget it in a grander victory than we have ever dreamed of.

No failure has been fatal, and no fault needs to be finally injurious, if your heart has been left undivided and your love is still loyal to your Lord, and you can answer back from the depths of your being, *"Lord; thou knowest that I love thee"* (John 21:15)! It is not the vibration of the trembling needle that He watches but its trend steadfastly toward the pole, and the fact that it can rest only when it points without wavering in that direction.

For such He has a precious service, and the three commissions given to the great apostle are also left for us in the largest measure in which our love will take them up and faithfully fulfill them. *"Feed my lambs"* (John 21:15) is His call to the ministry of salvation, the finding of His lost ones and the nurturing of His little ones. "Shepherd my feeble sheep" (see John 21:16) is His call to the still tenderer ministry of sympathy, instruction, sanctification, and healing to which He sends us forth for the multitudes in His church who are weak and broken in their Christian lives and longing sincerely for a more satisfactory Christian experience. *"Feed my sheep"* (John 21:17) is His call to labor for the most advanced Christians whom our own experience of the truth and the Lord may qualify us to help. But for all these, the chief qualification is a heart of love for the person of Christ; without it, all our words and works are *"sounding brass, or a tinkling cymbal"* (1 Corinthians 13:1).

5. We Are Called to Follow Jesus, No Matter What His Plan for Us Is

There is a final lesson that is a very humbling one but very necessary: *"If I will…, what is that to thee? follow thou me"* (John 21:22; see verses 18–21). This lesson silences our self-sufficiency and takes our eyes off of all other people. It leaves each of us alone with that Blessed One who passes from our view not only as the gentle, loving Christ but also as the mighty and eternal Sovereign of our life, with a supreme right to command our every choice and with a claim over each of us for the answering cry of Mary at the open tomb (see John 20:16)—the cry of absolute surrender, self-renunciation, and entire consecration. Oh, let each of us send that cry back as our answer to this solemn message right now, as we say, "Rabboni, my Master, I will follow You wherever You lead!"

6

THE GREAT COMMISSION

"And Jesus came and spake unto them, saying,
All power is given unto me in heaven and in earth.
Go ye therefore, and teach [disciple] all nations, baptizing
them in the name of the Father, and of the Son,
and of the Holy Ghost: teaching them to observe all things
whatsoever I have commanded you."
—Matthew 28:18–20

The manifestation of the Lord Jesus recorded at the end of Matthew 28 was, in some respects, the most remarkable of all His appearances during the forty days. It was the only one by special appointment, the others being merely incidental and mostly unexpected. This meeting He had arranged for even before His crucifixion, saying to His disciples, *"After that I am risen, I will go before you into Galilee"* (Mark 14:28). And this had been the message of the angel to the women on the morning of His resurrection: "*Go quickly, and tell his disciples that he is risen from the dead; and, behold, he goeth before you into Galilee; there shall ye see him: lo, I have told you*" (Matthew 28:7). This was also the direct message of Christ Himself as He first met the women returning from the sepulcher: "*Go tell my brethren that they go into Galilee, and there shall they see me*" (Matthew 28:10).

This, then, had been the special appointment for His great meeting with all His disciples, and it seems a little strange, in view of the urgency and emphasis with which the message had been given, that they were so slow in obeying it and in meeting their appointment with Him. They tarried in the neighborhood of Jerusalem for at least eight days after the resurrection, for there were certainly two Sabbaths in immediate succession in which He appeared to them there. Were they waiting for Thomas to join their number, or were they needlessly tardy in beginning their journey? Perhaps, the cause of the delay was in order that all the disciples might receive the message and have time to attend the solemn convocation.

We are not told the appointed place, but it was a mountain in Galilee. It would scarcely be Mount Hermon, the Mount of Transfiguration, for that would be more remote and difficult to access than was necessary. It may have been the same mountain where the sermon of Matthew 5 was delivered, the famous Horns of Hattin, where Jesus had first proclaimed the principles of His kingdom to the world. It is probable that the "*five hundred brethren*" of whom Paul spoke in 1 Corinthians 15:6 as having all seen Him together were the persons present at this gathering. They formed the surviving few who still remained faithful after all the tragedy of the crucifixion.

Finally, they have come together and are waiting for His appearing. It was the first great missionary convention that the world ever held, and it is most remarkable that the only appointment that Jesus made with His disciples after the resurrection was a missionary one. What a solemn emphasis it gives to the Great Commission and the glorious work of evangelizing the world, to fully realize the dignity with which Christ has invested this great occasion!

Then, the Lord appears in their midst. His coming to them seems to have differed in the form of its manifestation from any of His previous appearances. The Greek word translated *"came"* in the phrase *"came...unto them"* (Matthew 28:18) has a special shade of meaning, implying a gradual approach—"He came toward them," becoming visible at first at some distance and majestically coming nearer, until at last He stood before them, coming down, perhaps, from the lofty mountaintop that rose above their heads. His appearance was impressive enough to throw most of them upon their faces in adoring reverence. Yet there were some, even there, who doubted Jesus' identity. (See Matthew 28:17.)

Then, He addressed to them His great and important message, containing, first, the claim of His kingly power and prerogatives; second, His Great Commission to them to go forth and establish His kingdom among all nations; and third, the promise of His presence through all the days until the end of the age. As we dwell upon these three great themes, let us realize that this was not a message to the eleven alone but to all the disciples of Jesus Christ, to all the days until the end of the age. The company He had in His mind's eye must have included all who gathered around Him and would take up His commands, even unto the end of the age of which He spoke. It included us, if we will meet the conditions of His promise and the responsibilities of His great command.

The Royal Proclamation: "All Power Is Given Unto Me"

Jesus said, *"All power is given unto me in heaven and in earth"* (Matthew 28:18). This is really the manifesto of our King in assuming His mediatorial throne. In declaring that all power is given unto Him in heaven and in earth, He does not refer to His primordial deity and His divine rights but to that special kingdom and authority given to Him in the eternal covenant of redemption on account of His finished work. It is something that has now been given to Him; it is the throne of the Mediator that He assumes at the Father's right hand, for the purpose of accomplishing His great work of redemption, for which He has already suffered and died. It is that of which He declared: *"The Father… hath committed all judgment unto the Son"* (John 5:22). *"The Father loveth the Son, and hath given all things into his hand"* (John 3:35). Jesus must reign until *"he hath put all things under his feet….Then shall the Son also himself be subject unto* [the Father] *that put all things under him,"* to whom He shall deliver up the kingdom, and *"God* [shall] *be all in all"* (1 Corinthians 15:27–28).

The word *"power"* in Matthew 28:18 more exactly means "dominion, authority" and refers to the scepter and sovereignty of a king. The Lord Jesus means that He has been appointed to administer the government of both heaven and earth until the consummation of redemption. It is, indeed, a glorious and transcendent claim.

Facets of Jesus' "All Power"

1. Jesus Has All Power over All People

The risen Christ has all power to settle the standing and destiny of every sinner, and to control all of a believer's future prospects and relations to God. Jesus Himself could say to the Father, "*Thou hast given him* [the Son] *power over all flesh, that he should give eternal life to as many as thou hast given him*" (John 17:2). Through His name and the acceptance of His words, all sins are forgiven, and the guilty soul is translated in a moment out of the kingdom of Satan and from the curse of sin and hell to the "*glorious liberty of the children of God*" (Romans 8:21) and to heirship of His everlasting kingdom. Jesus has the power to arrest the sentence of judgment and condemnation in a moment, and to proclaim the guilty acquitted, justified, and a joint-heir with Himself of all the hopes of the gospel. (See Romans 8:17.)

The power of salvation is in Jesus' hands. Once, when visiting the Castle of Toulon in France, the emperor gave to a friendly king the right to set a single prisoner free, and he accepted it as a royal compliment. But the Son of God has received from the Father the right to emancipate every criminal under the sun from every curse of the law of God, if the criminal will accept His mighty clemency. Well may we rejoice in the power of Jesus—His power to save. Well may the prophet cry in wonder and admiration, "*Who is this that cometh from Edom, with dyed garments from Bozrah?...I that speak in righteousness, mighty to save*" (Isaiah 63:1).

2. Jesus Has All Power to Control the Power of the Holy Spirit

The mighty Spirit of Pentecost is Jesus' gift. The power that convicts of sin, of righteousness, and of judgment is from Him. (See John 16:8.) The power that clothed the apostles with such resistless might and divine efficiency is the power of our risen Christ, for Peter said of Him,

> *Being by the right hand of God exalted, and having received of the Father the promise of the Holy Ghost, he hath shed forth this, which ye now see and hear....Therefore let all the*

*house of Israel know assuredly, that God hath made this
same Jesus, whom ye have crucified, both Lord and Christ.*
(Acts 2:33, 36)

"God giveth not the Spirit by measure unto [Jesus]*"* (John 3:34).
Jesus still has power to awaken the most insensible soul and
break the most hardened heart. It was He who struck down Saul
of Tarsus and broke his heart by a glance and a word. It was He
who convicted the heathen jailer in the midnight hour. It was He
who opened the heart of Lydia as the sun opens the blossoms of
spring. (See Acts 16:13–15.) And He still has power to draw the
sinner, to melt the stony heart, to conquer the stubborn will, to
sanctify the sinful soul, to consecrate the whole being to Himself.

Is there anything that we need in our own spiritual life or in
our work for souls? Our glorious King has all power in heaven
and in earth to accomplish it.

3. Jesus Has All Power to Give Efficacy to Our Prayers

Jesus is our Great High Priest, as well as our King. The
Father always hears Him. (See, for example, John 11:42.) Jesus'
hands receive our imperfect supplications, cleanse them from
their defects, and add to them His own intercessions and the
incense of His perfect offering; and then He claims them as
the right of His redemption and fulfills them by the might of
His omnipotence. Thus, there is nothing too hard for Him to
grant to our supplications or too difficult for us to ask of His
almighty faithfulness, when we remember that we are presenting
our requests in the very name and character of Him who has *"all
power...in heaven and in earth"* (Matthew 28:18). *"Seeing then that
we have a great high priest, that is passed into the heavens, Jesus the
Son of God, let us...come boldly unto the throne of grace"* (Hebrews
4:14, 16). As we go forth in our work for God, especially in fulfillment of the Great Commission of this passage, our weapon is

chiefly prayer. And in the light of this mighty manifesto, what may we not dare to claim for our own efficiency and the evangelization of the world?

4. Jesus Has All Power in the Realm of Providence

The mighty and burning wheels of Ezekiel's vision all move at the touch of His hand (see Ezekiel 1:15–21); the chariots of Zechariah's vision, which rode through the earth and put all its conflicts to rest, go forth at His bidding (see Zechariah 6:1–7). The thrones of earth rise and fall at His command. The events of history are the outworking of His plans. The book with the seven seals is held by His hand and opened by Him alone. (See Revelation 5:1–5.)

It is not true, of course, that He is responsible for the wickedness and willfulness of man; but His hand is over all of man's ways, and His providence rules over all events. We see this constantly in His earthly ministry and in His government of the church in the Acts of the Apostles. How easily He could send Peter to the sea for the single fish that had the golden coin in its mouth, sufficient to meet His needs! How exactly He brought about the assembled multitudes at Pentecost, at the right time, to receive the Holy Spirit, and then scattered them all over the world! How wondrously He brought together Philip and the eunuch in the desert at the right moment, and then sent the converted prince to evangelize a kingdom and a continent! How easily He could lay His hand on the life of the impious Herod and protect the trusting Peter from his violence! How marvelously He guarded the life of Paul through perils of persecuting foes, through perils of waters and perils of every enemy, until his work for Him was accomplished!

How marvelously the Old Testament illustrates His providences! He could send the child of a Hebrew slave, who was doomed to death, into the house of Pharaoh to become the child of Egypt's king and the deliverer of Israel from the man who had sought his own life in infancy. He could lead an army of three million for forty years through the barren wilderness and sustain them without hunger or lack. He could send a Hebrew maiden into the house of Persia's monarch and make fair Esther the deliverer of her people. He could use Cyrus,[8] without his understanding it, to be the restorer of Israel's scattered tribes when the seventy years of exile were literally fulfilled, and make Daniel's captivity the occasion of his life and testimony in Babylon and the subjugation of Nebuchadnezzar and Darius at the feet of Israel's God. He could give Jeremiah courage to be fearless and faithful for forty years amid the perils of Jerusalem's last days, and then He could protect and guard his life alone, of all others, in the hour of her fall and amid the massacre of her inhabitants. And He who did all this is Jesus, our Lord and Christ, with power undiminished, who is waiting only for faith to claim its yet mightier victories in these last days.

What God wants today in His church and in His work is that the world will see not so much the power of the church as the power of her Lord and the presence of Him who goes forth with His weakest servants and becomes their might and their mighty Victor. Oh, as we go forth to evangelize the nations and to represent our God amid the mighty forces of the world's last and, intellectually, highest days, let it be our supreme mission to realize and show forth the might of our anointed King, and so to stand for Him that the world can see once more that He has *"all power...in heaven and in earth"* (Matthew 28:18).

---

8. Cyrus II, or Cyrus the Great, king of Persia and founder of the Achaemenian Empire.

God wants the world to see the presence of Him who goes forth with His weakest servants and becomes their might and their mighty Victor.

5. Jesus Has All Power over Natural Laws and Forces

The material world is Jesus' creation, and He does not usually mar or interrupt the uniform movement of the forces and laws that He has framed. Yet He can suspend them at will and substitute higher forces, if He pleases, just as the engineer can stop the engine or reverse it at his will. And so the Lord Jesus holds in His control the elements of nature. He can still quell the storm or bid it come; counteract the poisonous malaria or render it harmless; vitalize our exhausted physical frames with His divine life until "out of weakness they are made strong" (see Hebrews 11:34); and carry and sustain us through all the difficulties and apparent impossibilities that may surround our work for Him. Let us go forth, especially in the work of missions, realizing this: that nature is subordinate to redemption, that the natural is subordinate to the spiritual, and that the kingdom of matter is under the control of the King of saints.

6. Jesus Has All Power over the Minds and Passions of Men

On the mission field, Jesus can hold back savage heathens from their murderous design or render them helpless in their furious attack. Dr. Paton[9] tells us how often the savages of Tanna assembled to take his life, when some chief was led to

---

9. John Gibson Paton (1824–1907), Scottish Presbyterian missionary to the Vanuatu (formerly New Hebrides) islands in the Pacific southwest.

stand up in a critical moment and, by an unlooked-for suggestion, to turn them aside from their plan, and they dispersed
without hurting a hair on his head. And then again, even more
marvelously, how he had gone scores of times through armed
and furious crowds of naked savages who were determined
to murder him and had escaped their hands. Sometimes, he
turned to them and commanded them in the name of the God
of heaven to desist and disperse. Other times, he saw their
muskets pointed and their spears poised, but their weapons
fell unused to the ground in a few moments, and his life was
miraculously spared.

Our blessed Christ still has this power in every place
where His servants need His protecting presence, for He has
"all power...in earth" (Matthew 28:18). King's hearts are in
His hand, and He can still say to all our foes, *"Touch not mine
anointed, and do my prophets no harm"* (1 Chronicles 16:22;
Psalm 105:15). He can still induce men to receive us, to accept
our testimony, and to help us by their influence, their means,
and their cooperation. It was He who gave Daniel favor with
his masters in Babylon, Joseph the trust of Pharaoh, Mordecai
his place of power in Persia, and Paul the confidence of the
Roman captain and Caesar's household. And, in every age, He
has shown how He can put His hand on men when He needs
them and call them in a moment to the place He intends them
to fill.

Oh, that we might know our almighty King better and trust
Him more fully! Then would we trust less in man and care less
about either his frowns or his favor. Moving on in the might of a
divine dependence, we would know that God would bring to us
all men whom we need for His work and that He would help us,
by many or by few, as He sees best.

7. Jesus Has All Power over the Lower Orders of Creation

"*Behold, I give unto you power,*" Jesus says, "*to tread on serpents and scorpions,…and nothing shall by any means hurt you*" (Luke 10:19). He who went with Daniel into the lion's den has gone many times since then with men like Arnot[10] into the jungles of Africa and paralyzed the fury of the savage beasts and made them slink away abashed before the keen and fearless eye of His trusting child.

8. Jesus Has All Power over Satan and All Our Spiritual Foes

We are so glad of this truth. We meet our adversary with the assurance that he is a conquered foe in the presence of our Lord. We may well fear him in our own behalf, but as we claim the abiding presence of our Christ, Satan is but a toothless lion, a disarmed and humiliated foe, an empty shadow, and a sham. Let us not dread his power nor try to evade his fury, for he will do his worst against us. But with our Master in our midst, we need not be afraid; our adversary's assaults will only end in greater victories for us, and in all these things "*we are more than conquerors through him that loved us*" (Romans 8:37). Are we not sometimes afraid and shrink from positions where we know we will meet the adversary's wrath? Let us no longer dishonor our Lord but rather know that the places of the most peril are the places of the most absolute safety.

9. Jesus Has All Power over Angelic Beings

These mighty creatures who form the executive officers of the government of God and who throng the universe with their ceaseless ministries all go forth under the orders of our

10. Frederick Stanley Arnot (1858–1914), Scottish missionary.

anointed King. Myriads of them crowd this earth and wait upon the saints of God, but they are all subject to our Master's order. Occasionally, the curtain parts enough for us to see the shining form of one or two as they are engaged in their ceaseless services; but when we do not see them, they are doubtless always near.

The Old Testament is full of their interventions in human affairs, and the New Testament also has many examples of them. An angel opened the Redeemer's tomb; an angel told Mary of the resurrection; an angel opened Peter's prison and then smote his persecutor; an angel stood on the tossing ship by Paul's side and promised him deliverance.

And, surely, the ministry of angels did not end when the great apostles passed home. Unseen by mortal eyes, they have still fulfilled their loving tasks through every generation. And when each of us close our eyes on the last human face, we will find some shining companion by our side gazing upon us with a look of quiet recognition and tender affection, smiling at our look of wonder and saying to us, perhaps, "I have known you for half a century, better than your mother, your wife, or your dearest friend. I nursed your infancy, guarded your childhood, protected your manhood, hovered over your deathbed, and now am waiting to guide your spirit home."

Who of us cannot remember some moment when we had just escaped a sudden peril, stood within a hairbreadth of death; and as our palpitating heart recovered its pulsation, a strange heavenly hush breathed over our spirit and a voice almost seemed to whisper, *"He shall give his angels charge over thee, to keep thee in all thy ways"* (Psalm 91:11).

Samuel Rutherford[11] tells how he fell into a deep well when he was a child. For a long time, he struggled to hold on to the slippery sides and called in vain for help, and finally he began to sink. Just as he was perishing, he says, a beautiful man slipped quietly down into the well, lifted him out without a word, left him safely on the ground above, and immediately disappeared. The glorious old saint did not doubt that it literally had been an angel of the Lord.

We cannot tell how often angels have intervened for the visible deliverance of God's servants. Who knows but that they sometimes come in human guise, when all other help has failed? Enough to know that when we need them, they are at hand in the most lonely place, and that they are all under the command of the Son of God, for it is said, *"Let all the angels of God worship him"* (Hebrews 1:6). And in the book of Revelation, we see them going forth at His bidding to fulfill His mighty purposes in these last days.

10. Jesus Will Have All the Power of the Earth's Kingdoms Under His Scepter as the King of Kings and Lord of Lords

Our risen Christ is yet to have all the power of earth's kingdoms under His scepter and to be the King of Kings and Lord of Lords. God will overturn and overturn and overturn until He whose right it is comes, for "the kingdoms of this world must become the kingdom of our Lord and of His Christ." (See Revelation 11:15.) This is Christ's covenant right and reward, and the Father's heart will never be satisfied for His Son until His will be done on earth as it is in heaven. We will yet see our blessed King wearing the crown of the entire world, and we will

---

11. Samuel Rutherford (c. 1600–1661) was a Scottish Presbyterian pastor, theologian, and author who was part of the Covenanter movement. He was also the author of the noted political work *Lex, Rex*.

see every knee bowing to Him and every tongue confessing that He is Lord. (See Philippians 2:10–11.)

> He shall reign from pole to pole
> With illimitable sway;
> He shall reign, when, like a scroll
> Yonder heavens have passed away.[12]

Oh, let us realize the vision and hasten its fulfillment in His glorious coming!

The Great Commission: "Go and Disciple All Nations"

Because of Christ's power, and because of His right, He bids His disciples go forth to establish His kingdom among all nations.

1. The Command Is Bold and Majestic

We must be struck, first of all, with the boldness and majesty of this command. Jesus did not send His disciples simply to individuals but to nations. He looked upon the mighty communities of earth as not too great for the conquest of His kingdom and for the mission of His followers to win. He sends us forth as ambassadors to the earth's great powers and as His soldiers against the mighty hosts of humanity.

The work of foreign missions ought to deal very directly not only with individuals but also with nations. God has a purpose in the languages of earth. He wants them all represented in the great triumphant song that is to echo around His throne, and we ought not to be satisfied while a nation or tongue is not

---

12. James Montgomery, "Hark! The Song of Jubilee," *Evangelical Magazine*, July 1818, http://cyberhymnal.org/htm/h/a/harksong.htm.

evangelized. Indeed, His coming is directly connected with the evangelization of all nations, not necessarily all individuals. (See Matthew 24:14.) The church of today ought to lift up her eyes upon the fields and see how far and how faithfully she has fulfilled this commission with respect to neglected nations and unevangelized races and peoples. It would seem to be the special call of Christ to each of us today to see, so far as in us lies, that every community that has not yet received the gospel is specially visited with the message of our King. There are still many tribes of earth that have not received the message. There are scores in Africa and several in Asia who have yet no part in the chorus of redemption. And, if the Lord were to come tomorrow, their tongues would not be heard in the great millennial psalm that will arise at His coming, when

> All people that on earth do dwell,
> Sing to the Lord with cheerful voice.[13]

2. The Universality of the Great Commission Is Sublime

The Great Commission sweeps the circumference of the world. The kingdom of God spreads its royal scepter over an empire more magnificent than Nebuchadnezzar claimed or Caesar saw. It reaches far beyond the narrow limits of Jewish patriotism or imperial ambition. Never was there an empire so grand and universal as that which, by and by, will join in the chorus of coronation,

> [While] every kindred, every tribe,
> On this terrestrial ball,
>
> . . . .

---

13. William Kethe (attributed), "All People That on Earth Do Dwell," *Fourscore and Seven Psalms of David* (Geneva, Switzerland: 1561), http://www.hymntime.com/tch/htm/a/l/l/p/allpeopl.htm.

[Will] join the everlasting song,
And crown him Lord of all.[14]

Oh, as we have already said, let each missionary burn to make the victories of the gospel as universal as the commission that Jesus has given. And may each of us have the holy aspiration to add one other tongue or one other tribe that no one has reached before to the glorious song that is soon to burst forth when the ransomed hosts from every land will, with songs, surround the throne, and it will, indeed, be true that

Ten thousand thousand are their tongues,
But all their joys are one.[15]

3. The Great Commission Is Aggressive and Progressive: "Go ye."

The Great Commission does not imply, by any means, the idea of settling down in comfortable repose and consolidating great ecclesiastical institutions. It is a ministry of itinerance, and we very much doubt whether any church or servant of the Lord should cease to "go" in this sense of aggressive and progressive work. The missionary is to go until all regions are visited and all tribes evangelized; the church is to go until all who are at liberty have become the messengers of the gospel.

In the early church, we find not only Paul and Barnabas going but also Aquila and Priscilla, working people; Gaius and Aristarchus; and many of Paul's companions constantly moving with him from place to place. They were evidently men and women from the ordinary walks of life who counted it their commission

---

14. Edward Perronet (1779), adapted by John Rippon (1787), "All Hail the Power of Jesus' Name," *Hymns for the Living Church* (Carol Stream, IL: Hope Publishing Company), 1974.
15. Isaac Watts, "Come, Let Us Join Our Cheerful Songs," *Hymns and Spiritual Songs*, 1707, http://cyberhymnal.org/htm/c/o/comeletu.htm.

to share in the toils and tasks of the gospel. The time has come when the heathen world needs more than stereotyped ministers to meet its tremendous needs, and Christ is calling a whole army of plain and practical men and women to cover its needy fields. Good Bishop Taylor[16] has suggested the true method to a great extent. Good Pastor Hearns long before suggested perhaps an even better one, namely, the missionary colony. And today in Africa and India, thousands of happy native Christians are the fruit of a humble missionary movement in which a whole parish moved almost bodily to the heathen world and settled down among them to teach them how to live as well as how to know the Lord. May God grant that the next ten years may put such a *go* into the hearts of thousands of the consecrated children of God that they cannot stay at home any longer, and a great army of thousands of picked men and women, who fear no hardship and seek no rest short of the Master's coming, will spread over all the neglected fields of the heathen world!

4. The Great Commission Is to "Disciple" All Nations

The first process in this great work is denoted by the phrase "[disciple] *all nations*" (Matthew 28:19). It does not mean to "teach" all nations, which is an incorrect translation, but rather to evangelize and bring people into the knowledge of Christ and the fold of Christ. It is, in a word, the work of evangelization, the quick and worldwide proclamation of the gospel in every land, with a view to the gathering out of all who are willing to confess the truth and follow the Savior.

This is the first work of missions, and until this is done, the work of costly organization and education should be held in subordination. Too little has this been the object of missionary

---

16. William Taylor (1821–1902), evangelist, author, and missionary in the Methodist Episcopal Church and "America's first missionary bishop to Africa (1884–1896)," http://www.taylor.edu/about/heritage/bishop-william-taylor.shtml.

societies, and too much has been the building up of elaborate establishments. Some of the more recent societies have struck the true keynote and are sweeping over the world with a success unparalleled in modern missions. It is little wonder that the Master blesses a method so in keeping with His own command.

This was the apostolic method. In his great missionary journeys, Paul swept over vast fields. In a few months, he had itinerated over Cyprus, Iconium, and Central Asia Minor, and then was ready to go over those fields again and establish them more formally. On his later journeys, he swept with similar speed over Syria, Cilicia, Galatia, Macedonia, and Achaia in perhaps two or three years, preaching the gospel in many countries and gathering multitudes to Christ.

This is the world's great need today. In a single generation, its entire population will have passed away, and what has to be done must be done at once. It has been shown already that one thousand missionaries and two-and-a-half million dollars would evangelize the whole of China in five years; the same number of missionaries and the same amount of money would accomplish the same for Africa, provided that all sections of the continent could be safely penetrated—and God would undoubtedly open the way as fast as the church is ready to enter. The same number of missionaries and amount of money would cover all other neglected fields. A small army of picked men, with the trifling expenditure of seven-and-a-half million dollars, less than the fortune of many a Christian man, could evangelize the entire world long before the century is finished. And yet such a campaign would be sublimer, even if looked at only from a human standpoint, than any that the world has ever seen.

The Great Commission is to evangelize and bring people into the knowledge of Christ and the fold of Christ.

The other night, in Albert Hall in London, the royal family of England and the most distinguished men and women of the nation assembled and stood up on their feet to receive and honor Henry Stanley[17] because he had successfully penetrated Africa and rescued a brave man from isolation and peril. Oh, what honor will heaven pay to the men and women who will penetrate these dark regions for a nobler purpose and rescue their millions from the tyranny of Satan and the curse of despair! Surely all heaven will stand up some day to receive them, and the Son of God Himself will make them sit down and will serve them with His own royal hands. (See Luke 12:37.) May God help us to understand the meaning of our times and the magnificence of our opportunity!

5. The Work of Evangelization Should Be Followed by the Work of Organization

"Baptizing them in the name of the Father, and of the Son, and of the Holy Ghost" (Matthew 28:19). This is the ecclesiastical part, but there is a notable absence of all ecclesiasticism. We find no name of the modern church in this organization. The only name into which believers are baptized is that of God. Thank God the best missionary work of today is nondenominational! Thank God the churches of the mission field are growing weary of denominational names and finding it necessity to present to the colossal wall of heathenism the mighty front of the united church of Christ. And so, we find the "united church of Japan" and the struggle for the same united form in India and other mission fields.

---

17. Sir Henry Morton Stanley (1841–1904), British explorer.

There must, of course, be organization—such as the public confession of Christ in baptism, the uniting of the little flock in the name of Christ, and the proper discipline and government of the church—but this should be as simple and as like the early church as possible, and adapted in each case as to its form to the leadings of the missionary himself and the exigencies of the case.

6. The Great Commission Includes the Edification of the Church

The last direction respecting this great work refers to what we might call the edification of the church. It involves the building up of the church of Christ in truth and holiness. *"Teaching them to observe all things whatsoever I have commanded you"* (Matthew 28:20). This, of course, includes the deeper instruction and the higher training of the church of Christ; and this is proper and scriptural in both the church at home and the church abroad and should be carefully provided for, so that the flock may be fed not only with milk but also with meat, and prepared for the highest Christian living and the most effective work for the Master.

The church is not to be taught the traditions of men but the commandments of Christ; and not even so much the theological knowledge of the academies and school as the practical observances of His will and the duties and experiences of holy living, the one simple rule of life being His Word and His commandments.

How Have You Responded to the Great Commission?

Such, then, is the Master's Great Commission, the one message that He gave on this great occasion—this most important meeting with His flock after His resurrection.

Beloved, what have you done with this message? What are you going to do? What does this mean for you? You will soon meet Jesus in His kingly glory. What will you then say about this last word that He has left for you? Are you sure that you have an excuse that will meet His smile in that glorious day, and that He will say, "You have done your best to glorify Me and to accomplish My will for a lost world."

Unless we are sure we can meet Him thus, let us be very slow to take comfort in this last promise, *"And lo, I am with you always* ["all the days" AMP], *even to the end of the age"* (Matthew 28:20 NKJV), for it is very certain that it is linked with the commission and our obedience to it, as the Son is linked with the Father, and as obedience is ever linked with blessing. Unless I am sure I am doing more at home to send the gospel abroad than I can do abroad, I am bound to go. And if He wants me, I am ready to go whenever He calls and makes it plain. This and this alone is the attitude of fidelity on the part of each of us to this sacred word of our departing Lord. And with the most grave solemnity would we lay it upon the heart of every reader of these lines; and we feel sure that the Holy Spirit will carry it home with irresistible authority to the consciences of men and women, as the mandate of the Master Himself, to many who have not thought of it before.

Jesus' Abiding Presence

There is something very emphatic in the note of exclamation, *"Lo"* (Matthew 28:20)! It implies that the disciples would be likely to forget it. It is intended to call perpetual attention to it. No matter how improbable it may appear, or how many other presences may seem to crowd it out, yet *"Lo, I am with you"* (Matthew 28:20). Look more closely and you will see Him.

There is also special emphasis in the present tense: "*I am with you.*" Had He said, "I will be with you," it might have implied a presence different from what they now enjoyed—that there was to be a break in His abiding with them and then a subsequent appearing. But He says, in effect, "'*I am with you.*' I will not cease for a moment to be with you. I will be as truly with you the moment after My ascension as I am now while I am speaking these words to you."

It would seem as if the words "*I am*" had hidden in them an allusion to the Old Testament name that God used in speaking to Moses and in sending him forth to lead Israel from bondage to freedom: "*Thus shalt thou say unto the children of Israel, I AM hath sent me unto you*" (Exodus 3:14). Our Lord means to have us understand that He is the same almighty One who sent forth Moses to inaugurate the history of Israel, and who is now sending forth the disciples to inaugurate the history of Christianity.

What a blessed fullness that name suggests! It is an infinite blank that each of us may fill up with all we need Him for. "*I AM,*" He says, and we may finish the sentence. Is it health? "*I am the LORD that healeth thee*" (Exodus 15:26). Is it spiritual life? "*I am the living bread*" (John 6:51). Is it guidance? "*I am the light of the world: he that followeth me shall not walk in darkness, but shall have the light of life*" (John 8:12).

And then He tells us that He is with us "*all the days*" (Matthew 28:20 AMP)—not merely "always" but "*all the days,*" day by day, for each day's needs and duties as it comes, suiting His help and blessing to every changing day.

There is one more thought that lingers in the Master's last words with the light of a glorious hope. It is "*the end of the age*" (Matthew 28:20 NKJV). It points us forward to the second coming of our blessed Lord. It is very beautiful to see the blending of His departing and His coming in these words. Like the Northern twilight, which almost meets the opening of the dawn, so His departing and the hope of His returning blend in these blessed words.

Oh, how blessed to believe that the dawn is near and that already the daystar has arisen in our hearts (see 2 Peter 1:19), and the Presence that is now with us unseen is soon to burst upon us in the glory of His appearing!

7

THE LAST MEETING

"Ye shall receive power, after that the Holy Ghost is come upon you: and ye shall be witnesses unto me both in Jerusalem, and in all Judaea, and in Samaria, and unto the uttermost part of the earth."
—Acts 1:8

The scene of the previous two meetings with the risen Lord was Galilee. Now, we find Jesus again at Jerusalem, where the last of the forty days was passed. It is probable that those days were marked by many meetings as Jesus taught His disciples about the things concerning the kingdom of God with a fullness of which John said, *"If they should be written every one, I suppose that even the world itself could not contain the books that should be written"* (John 21:25).

Someday, we will know those unwritten words. Meanwhile, we may be sure that they were sufficient to authorize all that the apostles afterward did and said, and that while we may not have an actual word of Christ for all that we are expected to practice, we know that if we have the apostles' example for it, they had a sufficient word from His own lips. Thus, the observance of the first day of the week and many other things for which we have apostolic practice and example without explicit teaching were no doubt fully explained and authorized in the Master's patient and ample teachings.

So, finally, Jesus and His disciples meet for the last time. The interview is one of great importance, and the message is more distinct and far-reaching than any that had preceded it.

An Erroneous Question

All through these forty days, the disciples seem to have been constantly expecting Jesus to manifest Himself in the restoration of the old theocratic kingdom; and, again and again, as He met them and then vanished without fulfilling their expectations, they talked together and wondered why He did not publicly reveal Himself as the promised and kingly Messiah. At last they venture to ask Him, *"Lord, wilt thou at this time restore again the kingdom to Israel?"* (Acts 1:6). His answer is a very faithful and yet tender one. He does not rebuke them or even intimate that their desire is wholly without foundation in the purpose of God. He does not deny that He will restore the kingdom to Israel, but He simply turns them away from this expectation to their proper and present work and gently reminds them, with a shade of reproof, *"It is not for you to know the times or the seasons, which the Father hath put in his own power"* (Acts 1:7). Very solemnly does He hint to us that there are a great many questions with which we have nothing to do, and which are really keeping us back from our highest service for Him.

The Command to Wait in Jerusalem

Although Jesus had a practical and urgent work for His disciples to do, even this they were not to rush into unprepared but were to tarry for divine power to equip them for their great calling. He meant them to thoroughly understand that they were utterly unfit in themselves for the work to which they were called; that they must not attempt to do anything until they received the Holy Spirit, or they would surely do it amiss. And so, when they began to weary of the ten days' waiting, and, at Peter's suggestion, undertook to set in motion the machinery of the Christian church by electing a new apostle by lot (see Acts 1:15–26), their premature work simply came to nothing. The Lord quietly ignored their chosen apostle, and, in His own time and way, called Saul of Tarsus (Paul) to take the vacant place.

This is a lesson that none of us can learn too well. We are utterly unfit for the work of Christ by mere natural qualifications and preparation. All that we do before we receive the Holy Spirit counts for little or nothing. All our intellectual gifts, all our stores of accumulated learning, and all our experience and practice in Christian work will prove but cold dead wood on the altar of God until kindled by the heavenly flame of Pentecost.

There is a reason for this tarrying in the structure of the human mind. It prepares the heart for receiving the fullness of God. The spirit of waiting is a discipline of self-crucifixion and stillness that is necessary to the deep and full reception of the divine influence. And it is also true that at each successive stage of our life and work, and at each new departure, there must be a tarrying for power. God's first word to His people, as to Israel of old, is always, *"Stand still, and see the salvation of the Lord"* (Exodus 14:13), and then, *"Go forward"* (Exodus 14:15).

How long are we to tarry? Until we receive the power from on high. And when we do, we will not be able to tarry longer, but the fire in our bones, like Jeremiah's (see Jeremiah 20:9), will weary with forbearing and burst all barriers in testimony and service.

The Promise of Power Through the Holy Spirit

Jesus had already spoken of His power in heaven and in earth. Now He tells His disciples of the power in which they are to go forward and do His work. This power is different from that to which He had already referred in connection with His own person and presence, for it is to be in them and upon them as a personal enduement. And yet it was not to be *their* power but the power of a personal Presence that was to be in them, the true translation of Acts 1:8 being, "Ye shall receive the power of the Holy Ghost coming upon you."

There is a great difference between our receiving power from the Holy Spirit and our receiving the Holy Spirit as our power. In the latter case, we are as insignificant and insufficient as ever, and it is the Person who dwells within us who possesses and exercises all the gifts and powers of our ministry. Only as we abide in Him and He works in us are we able to exercise this power.

The Lord thus introduces to His disciples and to us that glorious Person who, ever since then, has been the substitute and successor of Jesus Christ in the personal life and work of every believer. There is no doubt whatever about Jesus' meaning in this passage and the importance attached to it. He is speaking of a divine and living Person, a Presence as mighty as the Father and the Son, as actual to us as the presence of Jesus was with the disciples of old. The Holy Spirit has been given to the church as the present God of the Christian dispensation, nearer even than the

Savior could be to His earthly companions, because He dwells within our inmost being and communicates directly with our innermost consciousness. He is the power for all true Christian work, and only as we are possessed and anointed by Him are we able to accomplish spiritual results that can be acceptable to Him or lasting in their effects.

The Holy Spirit is a Presence as mighty as the Father and the Son and as actual to us as the presence of Jesus was with His disciples.

The book of Acts provides the best examples of this reality. We need only look at Peter as he had been a month before, and Peter as he was on the day of Pentecost, to understand the promise and its importance. It was a power that imparted such heroic courage and boldness that the man who had fled from the servant girl (see, for example, Matthew 26:69–75) could now defy the whole Hebrew Sanhedrin and rejoice that he was counted worthy to suffer shame for his Lord (see Acts 5:17–42).

It was a power that illuminated the disciples' minds and enabled them to understand with marvelous clarity, and to expound with overwhelming conviction, the Scriptures and the gospel. Possessed with this power, Stephen could face the whole synagogue of the Cilicians, and they were not able to resist the wisdom and might with which he spoke. (See Acts 6:8–10.) And all the sermons recorded in the Acts of the Apostles are marked by the most marvelous depth and fullness of scriptural teaching and spiritual truth.

Additionally, it was a power that inspired the disciples with overcoming faith to claim the promises of God in all their omnipotence and to trust Him for His supernatural working amid all situations of need and danger. It was power to understand the will of God and know His guidance and follow His plan in founding the church of Christ on earth and fulfilling their various ministries. It was the power of love that made all their hearts one. It was the power of patient suffering that enabled Stephen and others to face their persecutors with a spirit that turned even their blood into a mightier witness for God than all of their words or deeds. (See, for example, Acts 6:9–8:8.)

It was the power to produce conviction and conversion in the hearts of men, the power that made men feel their sins, realize their need of a Savior, and accept Him. It was the power of supernatural and miraculous working that could rise above the laws of nature and the powers of disease and demonic possession, and work in the name of Jesus as Jesus Himself had worked. And it was the power that brought the providence of God to work upon their side, controlling the elements of nature and the great movements of human life so as to advance the kingdom of their risen Lord.

That blessed Holy Spirit is still the same unchanging power, and He is willing, in all our hearts, to work with His ancient might if He can find a vessel empty, cleansed, and yielded that will be fully responsive to His touch and will. Oh, let us tarry until we are endued with His power. And then, at each new step, let us tarry until we go forth in Him and in His perfect will and power!

The Purpose of This Enduement

"*Ye shall be witnesses unto me*" (Acts 1:8). This statement happily describes the work to which Christ calls His disciples. They are not to be the founders of sects and systems of theology, not to be witnesses of great principles and truths, but to be witnesses unto Him, to make Christ real to the consciences of men. Of course, He must be real to us first, for the witness can tell only of what he himself knows. This was always the great theme of apostolic testimony, and as we go back to it more fully in these last days, we will see the spirit of the early believers' piety revived. The church has too often been a great theological seminary rather than a place of simple testimony and the revelation and lifting up of Jesus Christ. Notice how, in all the disciples' addresses that are recorded, they invariably tell the whole story of Jesus! The words may be brief and few, but the story is fully told: His incarnation, His earthly ministry, His works of love, His mediatorial reign, His coming again, and His readiness to receive and save sinful men.

Someone has humorously said that the word *exegesis* might be slightly transposed to read "Exit Jesus"; and certainly a good deal of preaching is this sort of exegesis. But no messenger who goes forth with a loving heart to tell about Jesus and make Him real to sinful men will ever return with empty hands. This is the testimony God will bless. He wants it from our lips, and He wants it from our lives. He wants us so to speak and so to live that men will be conscious not of us or of our words but of Someone behind us whom they recognize by our testimony as the Source of all our life and the One who is just as willing to impart the same blessing to them.

Beloved, are we witnessing of Him in this way as we move among men or minister to others? Are we *"a sweet savour of Christ, in them that are saved, and in them that perish"* (2 Corinthians 2:15)?

The Scope of Their Ministry

The disciples' field was to be the world. Their plan of campaign was distinctly outlined. They were to begin at Jerusalem;

to extend their work among the scattered Jews through all Judea; to reach out next to Samaria, an intermediate race, kindred but not one with them; and then they were to embrace the entire Gentile world and carry the gospel to the uttermost part of the earth. Their commission, therefore, included the whole work of home and foreign missions, and most faithfully did they fulfill it.

Once again, the book of Acts is the best commentary on this verse, as it records the planting of the church at Jerusalem through Peter, James, John, and Stephen; the ministry of Peter and others to the scattered Jews; the work of Philip and others in Samaria; and then closes with the splendid sketch of the planting of Christianity and the inaugurating of the great work of foreign missions through the lips of Philip, Peter, and, especially, Paul and Barnabas. The larger part of the book is occupied with this last section, the gospel among the Gentiles. And over every section and every stage of this fourfold campaign, the Master's promise seems to hover as a cloud of glory: *"Ye shall receive power,…and ye shall be witnesses unto me"* (Acts 1:8).

So it was in Jerusalem, so it was in Judea, so it was in Samaria, and so it was in the uttermost part of the earth. At every stage of their wondrous work, it was manifest that the work was supernatural and divine. The power of God was constantly manifested in it, and His wonderful direction, protection, intervention, and blessing mark every page of the book of Acts and every step of their glorious work.

1. Witnesses in Jerusalem

Glance for a moment at their work in Jerusalem. How marvelously the power of the Holy Spirit came upon them! How simply and faithfully they witnessed unto Him before the multitudes at Pentecost, before the Sanhedrin as they were on trial, and before the cripple at the temple gate and the crowds that gazed upon his healing! How wonderfully God crowned their work with His power—the power that came in the tongues at Pentecost; the power that carried Peter's sermon home to the hearts of three thousand men and the multitudes that followed in the same work of faith; the power that smote the false Ananias and Sapphira; the power that rendered their persecutors incapable of refuting their words; the power that gathered the multitudes by the thousands into the infant church; the greater power that fused their hearts into a holy oneness and melted down all selfishness and worldliness in a heavenly flame of love and consecration; the power that enabled Stephen to speak to the learned and practiced sophists of the synagogue of Cilicia with a might that they could not deny; and then the power that enabled Stephen to meet their murderous hate with a face like an angel and a fortitude and love so sublime that the victory of his death was mightier than all the triumphs of his life, and the very man who had been chief witness against him was turned to God by his martyrdom and his dying prayer.

And so the whole story of the planting of the church in Jerusalem was the story of the power of the Holy Spirit and the testimony of Jesus through the lips of weak and humble instruments. The same power is still ready to crown our labors with success and to establish Christ's kingdom in our midst.

2. Witnesses in Judea

The same supernatural presence and power may be traced in the next stage of their work—the witnessing for Jesus through all Judea. The record of this work is chiefly connected with Peter. The story of his labors at Lydda and Joppa is but a sample page from the unpublished book of God's remembrance. The healing of Aeneas and the raising of Dorcas from the dead were not only mighty and majestic—the mightiest in the apostolic story—but were followed by still mightier results in the conversion of multitudes. We are told that *"all that dwelt at Lydda and Saron saw him* [Aeneas healed]*, and turned to the Lord"* (Acts 9:35). And of Dorcas's restoration it is said, *"It was known throughout all Joppa; and many believed in the Lord"* (Acts 9:42).

From the sacred narrative, we do not learn all of Peter's labors, but doubtless he carried the gospel, along with others, through all parts of Palestine, and it seems certain that he afterward visited Babylon and other places outside of Palestine where great numbers of his countrymen resided. We also know that Paul always presented Christ to the Jews wherever he went, and the little synagogue in every place became the nucleus and starting point for the entire community. God often worked wondrously among His own chosen people, before their brethren so rejected the truth that the apostles had to turn to the Gentiles.

3. Witnesses in Samaria

The gospel in Samaria was planted and established through the mighty power of God and the disciples' witnessing of Jesus. (See Acts 8:5–25.) The story begins, *"Then Philip went down to the city of Samaria, and preached Christ unto them. And the people with one accord gave heed unto those things which Philip spake, hearing and seeing the miracles which he did"* (Acts 8:5–6). The whole community seemed moved *"with one accord,"* and even Simon Magus, the wicked leader of a satanic ring of sorcerers and magicians, had to yield to the transcendent power of Jesus' name. We cannot withhold our attention from the fact that in this new aggressive moment of Christianity, the Lord Jesus sealed His word with signs and wonders; and we certainly have a right to expect such manifestations in every new stage of Christian work today, as well as such other times as His glory and truth require the special manifestation of His almighty presence.

> *Jesus sealed His word with signs and wonders, and we can expect the same manifestations in every new stage of Christian work today.*

But it was not the miracles that established Christianity. They simply awakened the attention and secured the confidence of the people; and then it was the power of the Holy Spirit upon the simple preaching of Jesus that brought the spiritual results in every case. It is most marked that after the acceptance of the testimony of Jesus, there was a personal baptism of the Holy Spirit upon the converts, bringing to them the actual and conscious experience of the Lord's presence and the salvation that they had claimed, and being to them an evidence that all the reasonings of man could never contradict and from which all the intimidations of persecution could not move them.

4. Witnesses to the Uttermost Part of the Earth

But the great work of the apostles was to be the planting of Christianity among the Gentiles and the witnessing of Jesus to the uttermost part of the earth.

Philip and the Ethiopian Eunuch

At a very early period in the book of Acts, we find the Holy Spirit leading out into the great work of missions. First, we have the call of Philip from his work in Samaria to meet the Ethiopian eunuch in the desert of Gaza. And this incident is as supernatural and marvelous as any of the steps that we have already traced, for over every step the message seems to reecho, *"Ye shall receive power, after that the Holy Ghost is come upon you: and ye shall be witnesses unto me"* (Acts 1:8).

It is the Spirit's call that sends Philip. It was a strange message. He was busy at Samaria, and the work never seemed so promising. But the call was imperative to leave this fruitful field and go down into a desert. It seemed the most unlikely place in the world to find work for Christ, or results that could repay such a sacrifice of time and labor, but he simply obeyed and went.

Beloved, let us remember that this was the founding of Christian missions, the first page in the wonderful chapter of the world's evangelization, and the pattern, therefore, for our missionary call. If we have received the power of the Holy Spirit and are called to the evangelization of the world, the summons will most likely come when we are otherwise occupied with work that it seems we must not leave. The call may summon us to what may seem a spiritual wilderness and the wasting of our energies upon a barren desert, as would seem to be the prospect for many a missionary who is plunging today into the heart of Africa or the remote regions of China.

But, lo, as Philip obeys, the desert becomes alive with the presence of God and the working of His mighty providence. The prince of Ethiopia, with all his train, is, at this very moment, returning to his land hungry, sad, and disappointed because he has not found the answer to his heart's deep questions or the light he is seeking upon the strange book he holds in his hands without being able to break the seal. The Spirit's work is not left half done. The message to Philip, "Go near, and join thyself to this chariot" (Acts 8:29), is quickly obeyed; and lo, a soul is saved, a new voice consecrated, and no doubt a mighty work of evangelization begun for the great continent to which the prince was just returning. And then, lest man should have too much to do with it, Philip is instantly caught away, and the eunuch goes on his way rejoicing, satisfied with his Master's presence and filled with the same Holy Spirit that had led Philip to him. (See Acts 8:26–39.)

So, the first Gentile convert was an African, and the first missionary to Africa was a native, and the power that brought it all about was the simple power of the Holy Spirit and the ascended Christ, working in methods and through instrumentalities that seemed weakness in themselves but that became *"mighty through God to the pulling down of strong holds"* (2 Corinthians 10:4). Similarly, we may expect His power to direct and confirm our efforts in His name to evangelize a lost world, as we dare to obey every call of the Spirit in humble obedience and simple faith.

Peter and Cornelius

The next chapter in Gentile Christianity is no less marked by the power of the Holy Spirit. It is the story of Peter and Cornelius. First, we see the Holy Spirit leading Peter aside for prayer, and then giving him a vision that prepared him to break through the old ceremonial barriers of Judaism and go among the Gentiles with the gospel. Next, we see the same Spirit working at that very moment in the heart of Cornelius and bidding him to send for Peter. Following this, we see the Spirit and the providence of God operating together as the messenger calls at Peter's house at the very moment that the Spirit has prepared him for the message. And then, like Philip, as Peter obeys and simply goes with the men to Joppa, we cannot fail to trace the wonderful working of God that had prepared the mind of this influential Roman for the gospel by all his previous history. In the same way, God is preparing the hearts of heathen men today and giving them a hunger that they do not understand but will make the gospel welcome to them when, at last, the messenger of Jesus reaches their land.

The message of Peter is true to the apostolic commission. He simply witnesses of Jesus. It is a wonderful message and tells the whole story of the gospel in as few words as were ever compressed into so short a space. It is the story of His life, of His death, of His resurrection, of His second coming, and of His gracious message of forgiveness and salvation to all who believe in His name. And as the witness was simply given, the Holy Spirit finished the work and fell upon the people in Pentecostal power. (See Acts 10.) And so, this might be called the second Pentecost and the inauguration of Gentile Christianity, corresponding with the planting of the church in Jerusalem. Here we have again a pattern chapter from the story of the early church. And why may we not expect the same mighty power to direct and confirm our work for the evangelization of the world, as we depend upon the same Holy Spirit?

The Establishment of the Church in Antioch

The next great step in witnessing for Jesus to the uttermost part of the earth was the establishment of the work in Antioch. It was necessary that there should be a new center for Gentile missions. The church at Jerusalem was too conservative and too much bound by the traditions of the past to be adjustable in the hands of God for so bold and worldwide a work. Therefore, the Holy Spirit called together, in the most simple and spontaneous manner, a company of simple-hearted, cosmopolitan believers who were free from all narrow bigotries and exclusive views. Many of them were laymen, most of them were provincial Jews or Gentiles, and they represented all social stations—from Simeon, the African; to Manaen, a courtier in Herod's family; to Barnabas, the princely and generous man of wealth; to Saul of Tarsus, the cultivated and profound philosopher and scholar. (See Acts 13:1.) They had just the elements to form a church of the largest sympathies and the most worldwide adaptations.

And so, without apostolic hands or ecclesiastical agency, the community of believers at Antioch just grew into a mother church, until the apostles heard of it and sent the right man to develop them without dwarfing them—the noble-hearted Barnabas. (See Acts 11:19–26.) And, before long, a new Jerusalem had grown up in Syria,[18] which God was henceforth to use as the mother of Gentile missions and the spring from which the waters of life would flow forth to the uttermost part of the earth.

And so today, it does seem that God is preparing new centers for foreign mission work. Tenderly but boldly, we are constrained to say that the ecclesiastical lines of our day have grown so rigid and the machinery of Christian work so elaborate and conservative that they have ceased to be fully adjustable to the world's great needs. Missionaries sent forth from such atmospheres carry with them to the foreign field the complexion of the home church, and they reproduce abroad the features that, in the church at home, neutralize her highest usefulness. And therefore God, in these last days, is gathering a great number of His consecrated children in all the churches into closer fellowship in Him, and from their midst is sending forth new missionary movements—nondenominational, independent, simple, and spiritual—that will carry to the heathen world the spirit of separation from the world, holiness of heart and life, entire consecration, self-sacrifice and simplicity in Christian living, and a full belief in the supernatural power of God and in the speedy coming of the Lord Jesus Christ, all of which must bring about a new phase of missionary life and work and a corresponding seal of the Holy Spirit upon the work and the workers.

---

18. Antioch was the capital of the province of Syria under the Romans.

Such, indeed, has been the case, and today scores and even hundreds of such workers, sent forth by no ecclesiastical body but by warm-hearted circles of consecrated men and women at home, are laboring, in the power of God, in many of the fields of Africa and China. Indeed, most of the effective missionary work of our time has sprung from such centers. The time has gone by for elaborate ecclesiastical missionary movements. We are in the day of spontaneous and simple Christian effort under the direct superintendence of the Holy Spirit and through men and women who are wholly baptized with His power. We believe most solemnly that the great movement today, which is calling together the consecrated children of God in every land in a closer fellowship of holiness and deeper spiritual life, is just the preparation of new missionary centers that are to cover the world before the close of the decade with an army of simple, self-denying messengers, through whom the whole world will be evangelized and the coming of our Master hastened.

The Calling of Saul of Tarsus

The last great agency in the evangelization of the world was the calling of Saul of Tarsus and his wonderful missionary life and work. Surely, above all else in the book of Acts, this is an expression of the power of the Holy Spirit. It was His power that called Saul on his way to Damascus, in a moment, to his Master's feet. It was His power that sent Saul (now also called Paul) forth as a minister and a witness, and clothed his lips and illuminated his mind with such marvelous messages and conceptions of the gospel. It was this power that trained him for his work alone in the deserts of Arabia (see Galatians 1:16–17) and taught his inmost spirit the secret of the Lord.

It was the Holy Spirit who called Paul to his great missionary work and who went forth with him into it at every stage as the directing Presence and enduing might of his own ministry. Mightily He stood by him in Cyprus as he confronted Elymas the sorcerer and claimed the soul of the governor for God. Mightily He vindicated His servant in the heathen mob of Derbe and Lystra as He healed the cripple and then raised up the apostle himself from the heap of stones, healed him of his bruises, and sent him forth to finish his work. Mightily He opened the hearts of the tribes in Asia Minor to receive the gospel and enabled Paul to plant the churches of Asia that afterward became such centers of life and power. With unerring wisdom and a strong Hand, that holy Presence guided him in all his plans, held him back irresistibly from Bithynia and Ephesus, and sent him over into Macedonia to commence his great crusade in the new continent that was afterward to become the chief theater of Gentile Christianity.

How supernaturally and triumphantly the Lord carried his servant through the perils of the Philippian mob; opened the soul of Lydia; and broke the heart of the Philippian jailer! How gloriously He defended Paul at Corinth from the fierce and treacherous foes who sought to destroy him, and gave free course to the gospel in that great metropolis of business and of sin! How divinely He led Paul at the right moment to the Oriental capital, Ephesus, and gave him his splendid triumphs there over the might of satanic power, and established the great church that was afterward to be the home of Timothy and John! How gloriously He led him forth to Jerusalem and to Rome, and carried him through all the perils of waters and of treacherous foes, until, at last, He enabled him, from a prisoner's chain in the Roman barracks, to so preach the gospel that the mighty Roman empire was shaken to its foundations and, before two hundred and fifty years had passed, was wholly turned to Christianity.

The great truth that we feel impressed to reiterate and emphasize, and that seems to shine out from our Master's message to His disciples, is that the work of the apostolic church was to be supernatural and divine; and, at every stage, the Master kept His promise literally and gloriously as they met His simple conditions: "*Ye shall receive power, after that the Holy Ghost is come upon you: and ye shall be witnesses unto me*" (Acts 1:8). The men themselves were as weak as we; the difficulties of their work far greater than our own. All the advantages of modern civilization and the means of transit to every portion of the world were lacking in their case. And yet, notwithstanding all, as they went forth to the Master's work in their weakness and simple fidelity, the cloud of His presence was as manifest as in the days of Moses or the campaigns of Joshua.

Why should it ever have ceased to be? Why should it not be restored again? Has the living energy departed from the promise? Has the Son of God grown old? Has His power or His wisdom decayed? Is the Holy Spirit exhausted with the centuries that have drained the ocean of His love and power? Or is He not waiting for the opportunity to manifest His presence and His might, and longing only for instruments and vessels through whom He can work with such simplicity that Christ can have all the glory, and that men will see not the workers but the power that works in them?

Oh, that we may tarry long enough to get right with Him and then go forth until He comes in His glorious exaltation and in His mighty name and power. And, perhaps, before our tarrying is over, some of us will find that we have been working without our armor and that we do not yet even know the Holy Spirit.

8

THE ASCENSION

"And when he had spoken these things, while they beheld, he
was taken up; and a cloud received him out of their sight."
—Acts 1:9

The last hour has finally come. The forty days are ending. He who has lingered so tenderly on the threshold of earth is ready to depart upon that journey from which we will someday see Him return. Tenderly has He chosen the sacred spot on which He will last look—the little home of Bethany. Perhaps, tenderly has He said farewell to its little home circle; or, it may be that they are in the company of His disciples at this hour.

He has just finished His last message. The sounds are lingering upon their ears, *"…unto the uttermost part of the earth"* (Acts 1:8), when lo! His form begins to rise. Not as before does He vanish into the impalpable air but visibly, distinctly, does He ascend before their eyes, gently borne upward without an effort.

As He rises, His hands are still extended in the benediction that He has just pronounced upon their heads. His face is lit up with tenderest love, and, no doubt, His gaze is fixed upon each in turn, with one personal and penetrating look of recognition and farewell that they will never forget.

Higher and higher He ascends, while they gaze as though they would go with Him if they could, until the strain is broken by a soft cloud that floats in between and hides Him from their view. But still the cloud ascends, and still they gaze upon it, until a voice awakens them from their absorbing view, and two angels by their side gently recall them to earth as they leave His last message: *"Ye men of Galilee, why stand ye gazing up into heaven? this same Jesus, which is taken up from you into heaven, shall so come in like manner as ye have seen him go into heaven"* (Acts 1:11).

It is past! The cloud has gone, the angels have departed, and slowly and solemnly they return to Jerusalem and wait for the next great chapter of Christianity: the descent of the Holy Spirit.

Christ's Ascension Referred to in the Scriptures

The scene that the disciples had been beholding is the theme of many an inspired picture. Two other allusions are made to it in the gospels. Luke referred to it with some further details in the closing verses of his gospel: *"[Jesus] led them out as far as Bethany, and he lifted up his hands, and blessed them. And it came to pass, while he blessed them, he was parted from them, and carried up into heaven. And they worshipped him, and returned to Jerusalem with great joy"* (Luke 24:50–52). Mark told us that *"He was received up into heaven, and sat on the right hand of God. And [the disciples] went forth, and preached every where, the Lord working with them, and confirming the word with signs following"* (Mark 16:19–20).

Some of the messianic psalms have shed a glorious light on the facts of Jesus' ascension. The Twenty-fourth Psalm sounds like a responsive chorus especially prepared for the angelic choirs that accompanied His ascension, the processional choir demanding as they approach the celestial portals, *"Lift up your heads, O ye gates; and be ye lift up, ye everlasting doors; and the King of glory shall come in"* (Psalm 24:7), while the chorus standing at the heavenly gates responds, *"Who is this King of glory?"* (verse 8), and the answering shout breaks forth, *"The* LORD *strong and mighty, the* LORD *mighty in battle. Lift up your heads, O ye gates; even lift them up, ye everlasting doors; and the King of glory shall come in"* (verses 8–9).

The Sixty-eighth Psalm tells us of the chariots of God and the twenty thousand angels that accompanied His ascension, and then it gives us the picture of the long procession of rescued captives from the prisons of Sheol, who followed His triumphal march and entered into the open heavens as the first company ransomed from the ranks of the Old Testament believers. Other conquerors marched in triumph with their captives dragged behind, but the only captives that graced His glorious ascent were those that He Himself had set at liberty. And then the psalm tells us of His ascension on high and His receiving gifts for men, so that the Lord Jehovah might dwell among them, which was fulfilled through Christ's ascension in the mighty gift of the Holy Spirit and the abiding presence of God with His people in the Christian dispensation. (See Psalm 68:17–18.)

The New Testament is full of this theme. Peter told the multitudes at Pentecost who saw and heard manifestations of the outpouring of the Holy Spirit, *"Therefore being by the right hand of God exalted, and having received of the Father the promise of the Holy Ghost, [Jesus] hath shed forth this, which ye now see and hear"* (Acts 2:33). And again he spoke of Christ's ascension, *"Whom the heaven must receive until the times of restitution of all things"* (Acts 3:21).

Paul referred to the ascension again and again in his epistles. In Romans 8:34, he said, *"It is Christ that died, yea rather, that is risen again, who is even at the right hand of God, who also maketh intercession for us."* In 1 Corinthians 15:25, he wrote, *"He must reign, till he hath put all enemies under his feet."* In Ephesians 1:19–23, he prayed that the disciples might know

> *the exceeding greatness of [God's] power…[who] raised [Christ] from the dead, and set him at his own right hand in the heavenly places, far above all principality, and power, and might, and dominion, and every name that is named, not only in this world, but also in that which is to come: and hath put all things under his feet, and gave him to be the head over all things to the church, which is his body, the fulness of him that filleth all in all.*   (Ephesians 1:19–23)

Paul told the Colossians that they were *"risen with Christ,"* and they were to *"seek those things which are above, where Christ sitteth on the right hand of God"* (Colossians 3:1). In Philippians 2:9–11, after describing the self-sacrifice and humility of Jesus, he added, *"Wherefore God also hath highly exalted him, and given him a name which is above every name: that at the name of Jesus every knee should bow,…and that every tongue should confess that Jesus Christ is Lord, to the glory of God the Father."*

The epistle to the Hebrews is full of this subject:

> *Who being the brightness of his glory, and the express image of his person, and upholding all things by the word of his power, when he had by himself purged our sins, sat down on the right hand of the Majesty on high.*   (Hebrews 1:3)

[God hath] put all things in subjection under his feet. For in that he put all in subjection under him, he left nothing that is not put under him.   (Hebrews 2:8)

Seeing then that we have a great high priest, that is passed into the heavens, Jesus the Son of God, let us hold fast our profession. For we have not an high priest which cannot be touched with the feeling of our infirmities; but was in all points tempted like as we are, yet without sin. Let us therefore come boldly unto the throne of grace, that we may obtain mercy, and find grace to help in time of need.
                                        (Hebrews 4:14–16)

Later, the writer of Hebrews spoke of Jesus as the One who has *"entered…into heaven itself, now to appear in the presence of God for us"* (Hebrews 9:24), and declared that *"He is able also to save them to the uttermost that come unto God by him, seeing he ever liveth to make intercession for them. For such an high priest became us [*"was fitting for us"* NKJV], who is holy, harmless, undefiled, separate from sinners, and made higher than the heavens"* (Hebrews 7:25–26).

Peter spoke of Jesus as having *"gone into heaven,…angels and authorities and powers being made subject unto him"* (1 Peter 3:22). John declared that *"we have an advocate with the Father, Jesus Christ the righteous"* (1 John 2:1).

And finally, in the apocalyptic vision, we behold Christ again and again in His enthronement, grace, and glory. In the first chapter, we have a vision of Him as our Priest:

And in the midst of the seven lampstands One like the Son of Man, clothed with a garment down to the feet and girded about the chest with a golden band. His head and hair were white like wool, as white as snow, and His eyes like a flame

*of fire; His feet were like fine brass, as if refined in a furnace,
and His voice as the sound of many waters; He had in His
right hand seven stars, out of His mouth went a sharp two-
edged sword, and His countenance was like the sun shining
in its strength. And when I saw Him, I fell at His feet as
dead. But He laid His right hand on me, saying to me, "Do
not be afraid; I am the First and the Last. I am He who lives,
and was dead, and behold, I am alive forevermore. Amen.
And I have the keys of Hades and of Death."*

(Revelation 1:13–18 NKJV)

In the fifth chapter of Revelation, we behold Him as the
Priest-King, the Lion and the Lamb together, combining
almightiness and mercy, as He takes the book to open the seals
and administer the mediatorial kingdom. And in the nineteenth
chapter, we behold Him in His royal majesty about to leave the
heavenly throne and assume His millennial kingdom on earth.

Such are some of the scattered rays of light that shine from
the excellent glory upon the exalted person of the ascended
Christ. Let us gather up into a simple and practical focus some
of their lessons.

What Was the Purpose and Value of Christ's Ascension?

1. Christ's Ascension Was the Reward of His Sufferings and Obedience

What an eclipse those thirty-three and a half years had been!
What an awful descent for the Son of God! What a depth of
humiliation, what a strange baptism of agony and shame! What
an awful shadow of sin and the curse of a holy God and of a
broken law! Oh, how sweet heaven and home must have been to

His heart! What a divine and infinite joy to return to the bosom of His Father and His own primordial place of dignity and glory! Well might He say to His disciples, *"If ye loved me, ye would rejoice, because I…go unto the Father"* (John 14:28). Well may we join in the welcome home of our suffering Redeemer, crying,

Jesus, hail! enthroned in glory,
There forever to abide;
All the heav'nly hosts adore Thee,
Seated at Thy Father's side.[19]

2. Christ's Ascension Was God's Seal on the Finished Work of Redemption and the Final Token of His Full Acceptance of Christ's Great Sacrifice

Jesus had gone forth from heaven on a mission well understood, to assume the guilt of a fallen world and undertake the task of its reconciliation to God. He had stood on earth, under the eyes of God and of angels, and solemnly assumed in His baptism the sins of man. He had hung on the cross of Calvary, under the astonished gaze of the heavenly world, in the name of sinful men and in their behalf, as the embodiment of sin and the representative of lost humanity. Had He failed in His mighty task, He never could have entered heaven again as a Victor. But now we see Him returning in majestic triumph, all angels waiting upon Him in loving homage, and the Father setting Him at His own right hand in the place of the highest honor and kingly power. And we know that His work must have been accepted and His great undertaking gloriously accomplished, for He still occupies this place in our name and nature and takes His position not alone but in our behalf. Therefore, His glory is the seal

19. "Hail, Thou Once Despised Jesus," attributed to John Bakewell (1757) and probably altered by Martin Madan (1760), *Hymns for the Living Church* (Carol Stream, IL: Hope Publishing Company), 1974.

of our salvation, and all His triumph proclaims our triumph sure.

3. Christ's Ascension Was the Exaltation of Man to the Right Hand of God

It was as Man that Christ entered heaven and sat upon His throne. It is as the Son of Man, with a human face and form, that He is sitting there today. It is in our behalf that He has gone up to God. He claims our place there and keeps it till we come. What an honor to the once lost human race was the ascension of Christ! It was the entrance of a Man to the highest place in the heavenly world, with the firstfruits of this new race following in His train and taking a place with Him that angels could not claim. Lord, what is man that You have set Your heart upon him and so strangely redeemed and lifted him up forever? Oh, let us rejoice and shout for joy as we see the Son of God ascend and write our names upon the seats of glory, as our great Forerunner! God has recognized man's right to enter heaven, to enter it as a king, to enter its highest place of dignity and blessing through the ascension of the Son of Man.

It is in our behalf that Christ ascended to God.
He claims our place there and keeps it till we come.

4. Christ's Ascension Brought the Expulsion of Satan and the Settling Forever of Every Question Affecting Our Standing in the Presence of God

In the twelfth chapter of Revelation, there is a fine picture of the *"man child,"* born of the symbolical woman and caught up to the throne of God from the devouring fury of the dragon.

(See Revelation 12:1–5.) There is no doubt that this Man Child represents the Lord Jesus Christ, and the picture refers to His ascension. Revelation 12 continues with a description of the conflict in heaven that followed, and of the casting out of Satan and his angels. (See verses 7–10.) Satan had hitherto enjoyed access to the presence of God to accuse the saints, as we find him doing in the Old Testament in the cases of Job and Joshua the high priest. (See Job 1:6–2:6; Zechariah 3:1–2.)

But now the Advocate of the saints appears with the evidences of the settlement of all claims against them. He lays His own precious blood at the foot of the throne, and, by His finished work, claims the settling and silencing forever of every charge against them, and immediately the case is settled. The sentence of the Court is publicly declared, and the accusing counsel is dismissed forever. The case is over, and never again may a word of accusation be heard against them. The police of heaven are commanded to drive the accusers from the judgment seat, and Satan is hurled from the Holy Presence, while heaven shouts for joy, *"Rejoice, ye heavens,…for the accuser of our brethren is cast down, which accused them before our God day and night"* (Revelation 12:12, 10).

Henceforth, no charge against us can come to His ears, and all we need to keep us in victory is to apply this blessed verse: *"They overcame him by the blood of the Lamb, and by the word of their testimony"* (Revelation 12:11). If we are in Christ, we may truly "read [our] title clear to mansions in the skies"[20] and shout with the great apostle of faith, *"Who shall lay any thing to the charge of God's elect? It is God that justifieth. Who is he that condemneth? It is Christ that died, yea rather, that is risen again, who is even at the right hand of God, who also maketh intercession for us"* (Romans 8:33–34).

---

20. Isaac Watts, "When I Can Read My Title Clear," 1707.

5. Christ's Ascension Was the Beginning of His Work of Intercession as Our Great High Priest

This glorious ministry of intercession (see Hebrews 7:25) had been set forth by its most perfect type, the Hebrew high priest, as he entered into the Holy Place through the parted curtains of the mystic veil and represented the people in the immediate presence of Jehovah and beneath the Shekinah glory, which symbolized the Father's presence. Our beloved Lord was now to enter on this great ministry. It is of this that the Scriptures say: *"Christ is not entered into the holy places made with hands,… but into heaven itself, now to appear in the presence of God for us"* (Hebrews 9:24). *"Seeing then that we have a great high priest, that is passed into the heavens, Jesus the Son of God, let us hold fast our profession"* (Hebrews 4:14). *"It is Christ that died, yea rather, that is risen again, who is even at the right hand of God, who also maketh intercession for us"* (Romans 8:34).

The full significance of this work leads us into one of the most comforting and inspiring themes of Holy Scripture. As our High Priest, Jesus' business is to represent us constantly to the Father, to guard our interests, to keep us ever in the divine favor and fellowship, to cover all our sins with His precious blood, to render our persons accepted in His person and name, to present His merits and righteousness in our behalf, to offer our petitions at the throne of grace and claim our requests on His own account, and then to transmit to us the assurance of the answer by the Holy Spirit. He Himself asks for us ten thousand things that we know not enough to ask for ourselves, and He constantly guards our every interest with watchful and unsleeping love and care.

As our Great High Priest, it is His to deal with the whole question of our sins and failures, and to settle every matter respecting our salvation and our spiritual interests. It is His to be *"touched with the feeling of our infirmities"* (Hebrews 4:15), to sympathize with our sorrows, and to send us comfort and relief in time of need. This intercession is most tender, unceasing, and personal. Like Aaron the high priest, who bore the tribes of Israel engraved upon his shoulders and upon his breastplate, so Jesus bears us individually upon His heart and upon His hands, and holds us up as part of Himself to His Father's love and blessing evermore.

> Where high the heavenly temple stands,
> the house of God not made with hands,
> a great High Priest our nature wears,
> the Guardian of mankind appears.
>
> He, who for men their surety stood,
> and poured on earth his precious blood,
> pursues in heaven his mighty plan,
> the Savior and the Friend of man.
>
> Though now ascended up on high,
> he bends on earth a brother's eye;
> partaker of the human name,
> he knows the frailty of our frame.
>
> . . . .
>
> In every pang that rends the heart
> the Man of Sorrows has a part;
> he sympathizes with our grief,
> and to the sufferer sends relief.[21]

Oh, may we not well rejoice in that blessed ascension that has given us such a Friend at our Father's side! It is not so much that

---

21. Michael Bruce and John Logan, "Where High the Heavenly Temple Stands," 1764, *Church Hymnary* (4th ed.), #451. See http://www.oremus.org/hymnal/w/w405. html; http://www.hymnary.org/text/where_high_the_heavenly_temple_stands.

the Father did not love us, or that we needed Jesus to appease an angry King; but we need this human channel of communion with the sovereign Deity and glorious Father, whom, apart from Jesus, we could never have known and never have dared thus boldly to approach. But in the name of Him who touches both God and man in His double nature, we are brought into union and fellowship with the Deity Himself, and we, *"who sometimes were far off are made nigh by the blood of Christ"* (Ephesians 2:13), and *"through him...have access...unto the Father"* (Ephesians 2:18).

6. Christ's Ascension Was Necessary for His Assumption of His Kingly Place on the Mediatorial Throne

Like Melchizedeck of old, Jesus is both Priest and King. (See Hebrews 6:20–7:3, 15–17.) His ascension has exalted Him to a literal throne of absolute sovereignty over *"all power...in heaven and in earth"* (Matthew 28:18). The Son of God today has supreme sway over all this mighty universe. He has ascended *"far above all principality, and power, and might, and dominion, and every name that is named"* (Ephesians 1:21) and has become *"head over all things to the church"* (Ephesians 1:22).

There is no natural law but is now perfectly subject to His control. There is no physical force but He can use or restrain at His sovereign pleasure. There is no created intelligence but He can move at His will or destroy at His command. His ascension has forever challenged the absolute despotism of natural law and physical force, and placed at the command of faith the highest force, which will be employed whenever His kingdom requires it, in defiance of every natural and ordinary principle. True, He does not ordinarily need to act in a manner contrary to existing laws and principles, any more than the entry of the young king of

Germany[22] upon the administration of the empire requires him to change the machinery of the government. He usually works in line with it but is always supreme above it. So the Son of God, sitting upon the throne of providence and grace, does not constantly assert His power by coming into collision with the existing machinery of the natural world but works in harmony with it and uses it for His own higher purpose.

But He is perfectly at liberty to suspend it and to contradict it when He so pleases. The ascension of Christ, therefore, has given us the right to expect His intervention, even to the utmost extent of the miraculous and supernatural, when the interests of His kingdom truly require it; and yet His power may be no less mighty when it is working along lines of perfect simplicity and naturalness.

Christ is King of nations. Strange as it may seem, for eighteen centuries, He has been controlling the dynasties and kingdoms of earth in accordance with Daniel's prophecy and along the lines that are to develop to His own second coming. Christ is King and Head of His church. He is King of nature and providence. His hand makes "all things work together for good to them that love God" (Romans 8:28). His power appears in every chapter of the story of the apostolic church. As I wrote earlier, we see Him working in the miracles of Pentecost, in Samaria, Joppa, Lystra, and Malta. We see Him opening Peter's prison and subduing Paul with one kingly glance of love and power. We see Him carrying the great apostle, as with a charmed life, through the perils of Asia Minor, the prison of Philippi, the mobs of Corinth and Athens, the murderous Jews of Jerusalem, the conspiracies that surrounded him at Caesarea, the wild Euroclydon of the Adriatic,[23] and even the

22. Wilhelm II (1859–1941), who became German Emperor and King of Prussia (1888–1918) at age twenty-nine.
23. Acts 27:14: *"But not long after there arose against it a tempestuous wind, called Euroclydon."*

terrors of the Colosseum; until, at last, the apostle could say, as he recalled that glorious Presence that had covered him with its shelter in all his marvelous life, *"The Lord shall deliver me from every evil work, and will preserve me unto his heavenly kingdom"* (2 Timothy 4:18).

Is Christ our King? Have we enthroned Him above every difficulty, adversary, and circumstance, and placed on His head many crowns? (See Revelation 19:12.) It was for this that He ascended. He holds the reins of universal power for our sake and on our account. He is *"head over all things to the church, which is his body"* (Ephesians 1:22–23). Not for Himself but for you and me does He sit above the circle of the stars and hold the reins of universal government. Oh, let Him be our Wonderful Counselor, our Mighty God (see Isaiah 9:6), and *"of the increase of his government and peace there shall be no end"* (Isaiah 9:7)!

Is Christ our King? Have we enthroned Him above every difficulty, adversary, and circumstance?

---

7. Christ Ascended to the Right Hand of God so that He Might Lift Us Up into an Ascension Life

Christ's ascension is the type of our highest spiritual life. Not only would He have us risen with Him from the death of the past but also ascended with Him over this present evil world and the power of the natural and temporal. For we are seated with Him in heavenly places, and we are to recognize ourselves as actually there, just as much as if the judgment was past, and we were already seated, in the ages to come, upon our kingly thrones.

This is a very important matter and the true key to victory in our Christian life. Everything depends upon the standpoint from which we look at things. Contemplating our troubles from our present apparent condition, they seem to be above us. But if we look at them as Christ sees them, and as we will see them in a little while, they will cease to alarm or distress us. Our faith will raise us above them and enable us to see them as more than conquered and simply as occasions for greater good and grander victory.

Climbing a cloud-encompassed mountain, a party of travelers became discouraged and begged their guide to take them down. They could not see a step in front of them through the mist that surrounded them with its damp and dreary folds, and they feared that they would lose their way and be involved in ruin. But the guide answered only, "No, friends, let us not go down, but let us go up a little higher, and we will be above the clouds." And, sure enough, a few bold strides in his footsteps up the steep declivity, and lo! the full sunlight of heaven burst upon them, and below them lay the billowy landscape of beautiful and many-tinted cloudland, a spectacle of glory.

And so the true victory over trial is to rise above it. A little higher, beloved, and you will dwell, like Joshua, in Timnath Serah, in the City of the Sun (see Joshua 19:50), and *"thy sun shall no more go down…: for the* LORD *shall be thine everlasting light"* (Isaiah 60:20).

It is possible to look at everything as Christ is looking at it, and to see it as you will see it when all is ended. It is possible to pray as Christ prays from heaven and to be conscious that our glorious Great High Priest is commanding and executing it from on high, and that all things must give way before His power and will. It is possible to recognize ourselves in the light of a few years hence, when we will be sitting with Him in the seats where our names are already written and our place prepared, and where God ever regards us as already seated.

Oh, what dignity and triumph this will give to the humblest career, and we will walk through earth as the children of a King, the *"heirs of God, and joint-heirs with Christ"* (Romans 8:17). For He who sits there is but the other part of our own life, and as we enter into closer union with His person, we will rise into the constant realization of His glorious power and learn to shout with the most tried and yet most triumphant of mortals, *"Who shall separate us from the love of Christ? shall tribulation, or distress, or persecution, or famine, or nakedness, or peril, or sword?…Nay, in all these things we are more than conquerors through him that loved us"* (Romans 8:35, 37).

Let Us Arise!

And now, beloved, the forty days are past. What have they been to us? How much more have they brought us into His living reality and ceaseless presence? And will they now lift us up with Him into a yet higher place of fellowship, exaltation, and victory? Let us arise! Let us ascend! Let us dwell on high! The veil is torn in two. The Holiest is open. The Holy Spirit is come. The heavens are opened, and the angels of God are ascending and descending upon the Son of Man. (See Genesis 28:12; John 1:51.) Come, O house of Jacob, and walk in the light of the Lord. (See Isaiah 2:5.)

> Go up, go up, my heart,
> Dwell with thy God above;
> For here thou canst not rest,
> Nor here give all thy love.
>
> Go up, go up my heart!
> Be not a trifler here:

Ascend above these clouds—
Dwell in a higher sphere.

. . . .

Go up, reluctant heart;
Take up thy rest above:
Arise, earth-clinging thoughts;
Ascend, my lingering love![24]

---

24. Horatius Bonar, "Go Up, Go Up, My Heart," 1836, *Amore Dei* (1897), #321,
http://www.hymnary.org/text/go_up_go_up_my_heart.

ABOUT THE AUTHOR

Albert Benjamin Simpson (1843–1919) was born to parents of Scottish descent and grew to become one of the most respected Christian figures in American evangelicalism. A much-sought-after speaker and pastor, Simpson founded a major evangelical denomination, published more than seventy books, edited a weekly magazine for nearly forty years, and wrote many gospel songs and poems.

The first few years of his life were spent in relative simplicity on Prince Edward Island, Canada, where his father, an elder in the Presbyterian church, worked as a shipbuilder and eventually became involved in the export/import industry. To avoid an approaching business depression, the family moved to Ontario, where the younger Simpson accepted Christ as his Savior at age fifteen and was subsequently "called by God to preach" the gospel of Christ.

Simpson went on to pastor New York's 13th Street Presbyterian Church. However, in 1881, he resigned and began to hold independent evangelistic meetings in New York City. A year later, the Gospel Tabernacle was built, and Simpson began to turn his vision toward establishing an organization for missions. Simpson helped to form and lead two evangelization societies: The Christian Alliance and The Evangelical Missionary Alliance. As thousands joined these two groups, Simpson sensed a need for the two to become one. In 1897, they became The Christian and Missionary Alliance.

Paul Rader, former pastor of the Moody Church in Chicago, once said: "[Simpson] was the greatest heart preacher I ever listened to. He preached out of his own rich dealings with God."

On October 28, 1919, Simpson slipped into a coma from which he never recovered. Family members recall that his final words were spoken to God in prayer for all the missionaries he had helped to send throughout the world.